Project Management for Lawyers

BARBARA J. BOAKE AND RICK A. KATHURIA

Globe Law
and Business

Authors
Barbara J. Boake and Rick A. Kathura

Published by
Globe Law and Business Ltd
3 Mylor Close
Horsell
Woking
Surrey GU21 4DD
United Kingdom
Tel: +44 20 3745 4770
www.globelawandbusiness.com

ISBN: 978-1-90778-761-4
A catalogue record for this book is available from the British Library

Contents

Executive summary

DURING THE economic boom that began in the late 1990s, legal services were in high demand. Most large law firms were able to dictate the price for their services and the manner in which they would be delivered without much regard for their clients' business requirements. The credit crisis put an end to this dynamic and put the buyer back in the driver's seat. Although there are signs of economic recovery, this shift in the lawyer-client balance of power is unlikely to change.

Clients are now in a position to do something about the disparity they see between the cost of legal services and the value of those services to their business. General counsel – many of whom spent their formative years in private practice – are familiar with the systemic inefficiencies that can exist in law firms and are unwilling to accept the status quo. They are looking for better value, more efficiency and lower costs. They are no longer prepared to bear the entire economic risk of the cost of legal work that may or may not produce the expected results. Alternative fee arrangements are becoming more and more common.

For a profession built around time-based billing, this presents a tremendous challenge. It requires a fundamental change in the way legal work is priced and managed. It also presents a clear opportunity for law firms or legal departments willing to invest in legal project management.

Legal project management provides a structured approach to planning, pricing and managing legal work that will bring a law firm's service delivery model in line with the changing expectations of its clients. It is a framework that allows lawyers to provide more reliable fee estimates, better matter management and improved matter profitability. In a highly-competitive, fixed-fee environment that is becoming the 'new normal', legal project management can be a law firm's lifeline.

This report is a practical guide for leaders of law firms and legal departments, who are considering legal project management as a way to deliver better value to their clients. It is also a useful handbook for individual lawyers who wish to improve their budgeting, planning and matter management skills.

Part One of the report will:

- Demonstrate the value of applying project management to a legal practice;
- Explain basic project management principles;
- Provide a simple legal project management framework;
- Describe tools and techniques to support the framework;
- Discuss legal project management as a pricing strategy; and
- Share practical advice on how to develop and implement a legal project management programme in a law firm or legal department.

As with any new initiative that requires a significant investment of resources, a business case for legal project management must be made. Chapter 1 discusses the value of legal project management in the changing legal market. The misalignment between the way law firms have traditionally worked and the way clients run their businesses will become clear. The increasing size and sophistication of in-house legal departments, the growth of legal outsourcing and the increasing popularity of alternative fee arrangements have had a significant impact on the sustainability of the full-service law firm model. These market factors are discussed in detail and a compelling business case for legal project management is made.

Project management is a well-developed discipline that uses a wide variety of complex tools and techniques. The key to introducing project management to lawyers is to adopt only those principles that are simple and useful enough to be embraced by a practising lawyer. Chapter 2 describes the basic project management principles upon which the report's legal project management framework is based. The triple constraints of scope, time and cost that are common to all projects are examined. The project life cycle is explained and the five key project management processes are identified.

The project management principles discussed in Chapter 2 are incorporated into a simple legal project management framework in Chapter 3. The framework begins with the proposition that legal mandates are projects and can be managed accordingly. Lawyers are now expected to accept a dual responsibility for performing the legal work and managing the work within a budget. A legal project management framework provides a context within which this dual role can be performed.

The framework divides a legal matter into its component project parts (as opposed to its substantive legal parts) as follows:

- Define;
- Plan;
- Monitor; and
- Evaluate.

Each component of the legal project management framework is discussed in detail in chapters 4, 5, 6, 7 and 8. In addition, the legal project management skills, tools and techniques that support this framework are described.

The application of legal project management to pricing strategies is discussed in Chapter 9, including ways that it can contribute to overall firm profitability.

After the legal project management framework has been fully explained, guidance is provided in Chapter 10 on how to design and implement a legal project management programme in a law firm or legal department. Understanding that each firm will have its unique culture, the report provides practical advice on setting objectives, finding the right resources and managing change.

The case studies found in Part Two of this report provide examples of US, UK and Canadian law firms that have designed and implemented legal project management programmes successfully in their organisations. A case study from a large international financial institution is featured to provide a client's perspective on the value of legal project management and the way in which it will become the new standard for all law firms with whom it deals worldwide.

About the authors

THIS REPORT is a compilation of knowledge, best practices and lessons learned by two individuals with different but complementary backgrounds.

Barbara Boake is a senior partner at McCarthy Tétrault LLP, practising in the areas of bankruptcy, insolvency and restructuring. With over 20 years of practice experience and having served on her firm's board of partners and its executive team, Barbara was named one of the 'Top 100 Most Powerful Women' in Canada by the Women's Executive Network. While a member of her firm's executive team she was responsible for leading the development and implementation of the firm's 'Dialogue Project Management™' programme. Barbara speaks regularly on all aspects of project management for the legal profession.

Rick Kathuria is a professional engineer, certified management consultant and a certified project management professional with over 15 years of experience working on large international projects at top tier consulting firms, before starting his own consulting firm. His projects included managing multimillion dollar projects internationally, as well as the implementation of internal project management offices for several of his clients. He also serves in a leadership role in operating the Project Management Institute's 'Legal Project Management Community of Practice'. He has been working with McCarthy Tétrault LLP as head of its IT development group and director of its project management office, where he oversees major implementation projects. He has spent the last few years working with senior partners of the firm to develop project management training and he designed the tools that they are currently using. In this capacity, he was also responsible for delivering training to lawyers and providing ongoing coaching to help them effectively project manage their legal mandates.

Both authors began with a blank slate and created a legal project management programme that is changing the way the firm's lawyers plan, price and deliver legal work. This report is a guide through this challenging, but very rewarding process.

Barbara Boake can be contacted at: bboake@mccarthy.ca and Rick Kathuria at: rkathuria@mccarthy.ca or lpm.servicedelivery@vcleader.pmi.org.

PART ONE

Legal Project Management Best Practice – A Framework, Tools and Techniques

Chapter 1: The business case for project management

The shift in the balance of power from seller to buyer

Much has been written about the changing market for legal services. There is a range of views, from predictions about our profession's imminent demise,[1] to more moderate assessments of the short-term impact of the economic downturn.

There is no doubt that the legal services market is changing and the important question is why this is happening. If the new demands of the market amount to nothing more than short-term price pressure arising from a challenging economic environment, we can assume that the pendulum will begin swinging back, particularly now that we are seeing signs of economic recovery. However, a close examination of what is really behind these changes suggests that the recession was merely a catalyst for an inevitable shift in the balance of power from seller to buyer that will have a long-term impact on the way lawyers work. The boom experienced by the legal profession in the decade leading up to the recession created an environment in which law firms – and not clients – were dictating the way legal services would be priced and delivered. This is a most unusual dynamic in a service business, and it cannot reasonably be expected to continue.

Embracing business realities

There is a misalignment between the way law firms work and the way clients work, and a failure to address this disparity is a strategic mistake.

Consider the following three characteristics of the legal profession and the extent to which they are misaligned with the business objectives of most buyers of legal services.

Time-based billing

Businesses are constantly looking for ways to improve efficiency in order to reduce costs and increase profits. Law firms, on the other hand, do not need to be efficient in the provision of their services to be profitable. Since law firm revenue depends on generating billable hours, utilisation is a major profitability driver. But efficiency is not.

In most law firms, compensation and promotion are typically linked in one way or another to the number of billable hours that lawyers generate for themselves or others. The incentive to generate billable hours is obvious and the risk that this could lead to cost inefficiencies has historically been borne by our clients.

At the risk of stating the obvious, clients prefer pricing models that encourage, not discourage, efficiency.

Annual rate setting

Generally, hourly rates are the product of a firm's own costs, plus a profit margin. This is why the legal profession is sometimes referred to as a 'cost-plus' business. Individual rates generally increase each calendar year, on the assumption that lawyers become more valuable with each year of experience. While this may be true, it does not take into account the real value of the work to the client. Although many law firms will conduct market research when setting rates, it is often limited to an investigation of what competing law firms are charging for lawyers with similar year of experience.

In the period leading up to the recession, the cost-plus business model led to an unprecedented period of growth and profitability for large law firms around the world. Legal services were in high demand and growing salary, space and technology costs drove rates up every year. The price of legal services increased substantially and a backlash was inevitable.

Unpredictable overall costs

Corporate clients run their businesses according to budgets, with strict accountability for cost overruns. They typically receive pricing from their suppliers that is transparent and predictable.

The law firm practice of setting the meter at the beginning of a mandate and charging whatever amount is displayed at the end is at odds with this fundamental requirement of good financial management. Although fixed-fee pricing is becoming more common in certain areas of legal practice, the legal profession as a whole appears to be lagging behind other professional services in adapting its pricing models.

Accounting and consulting firms have adjusted their compensation systems and pricing policies over the years to bring them more in line with the needs of their clients. In the consulting industry, more attention is given to the expected cost of a project, since there is often a threshold decision to be made as to whether the project is worth undertaking. A cost-benefit business case is a standard requirement. If the project is mandatory or critical to the business, as is frequently the case in legal matters, this dynamic can change. For example, in the late 1990s when the business world was concerned with the impact of 'Y2K', IT consulting firms had the ability to simply turn on the meter and begin charging. Shortly after 'Y2K', this market reverted back to a very cost-conscious environment, where companies looked long and hard at the cost-benefit analysis before approving a project. The parallels to the post-boom legal profession are clear.

It is not reasonable to assume that the legal profession can continue to be an outlier. Time-based billing, arbitrary annual rate setting and the lack of transparency and predictability in pricing are being questioned by an increasingly sophisticated market. A client's perspective on this is provided in Case study 5.

One very good reason to consider project management is that it will enable a law firm to align itself more closely with its clients' interests, and this will result in a service delivery model which is more in line with client expectations and business realities.

The growth of in-house legal departments

With the increasing size and sophistication of internal legal departments, law firms are playing a less essential role in the business of their clients and are looking more and more like other professional service providers. In this role, it becomes more difficult to justify a service delivery model that is unique.

Many of the individuals who now lead in-house legal departments would have spent some part of their careers in private practice, and so would have a very good understanding of the cost-plus model and the various ways it can work to a law firm's advantage. They would also have a unique perspective on the dramatic increase in profits per partner enjoyed at most firms during the boom years. They might reasonably question their own role in tolerating this trend and believe it to be in the best interests of their organisation that they address this apparent imbalance. And that is precisely what they are doing.

The Association of Corporate Counsel (ACC) is the largest organisation of in-house counsel in the world. It has over 25,000 members, representing over 10,000 organisations in 75 countries. The ACC recently surveyed its members to determine what general counsel valued most in its external legal providers and this is what it found:

- Better management, lean efficiency;
- Certainty/predictability;
- Focus on outcomes and results, not just process and analysis;
- Costs that equate with value received; and
- Outside counsel and firms whose motivations and business model are aligned with the client's.[2]

Having identified a gap between what its members expected and what they were in fact experiencing, the ACC issued its 'Value Challenge'. In essence, this is a challenge to law firms to increase the value and reduce the cost of their services (without impacting their profitability). It is also a challenge to in-house counsel to collectively drive this change.

One of the tools that the ACC developed to assist its members in this effort is the 'ACC Value Index'. This is an online review of law firm performance on a five-point scale (with one being the lowest score and five being the highest). The firms are rated on the following criteria:

- An understanding of objectives/expectations;
- Legal expertise;
- Efficiency/process management;
- Responsiveness/communications;
- Predictable costs/budgeting skills; and
- Results delivered/execution.

The results are available to all ACC members. The 'Value Index' is relatively new and the impact on a law firm's business remains to be seen. However, given that the 'ACC Value Index' scores are available to some of the most influential corporate counsel in the world, it clearly does have the potential to play a significant role. In any event, the introduction of accountability on metrics such as budgeting, cost predictability, efficiency and matter management should increase the pressure on law firms to improve their skills in these areas.

In a market that is demanding predictability, efficiency and cost control, law firms must focus on matter management skills to stay competitive. Project management is typically not taught in law schools and while lawyers are generally adept at managing complex legal work, budgets are something most will avoid if possible. Project management can provide the tools and training necessary for lawyers and other legal professionals to perform well in this new environment.

The fragmentation of the legal services market

Globalisation and advances in technology have allowed new entrants into the legal services industry in the form of legal outsourcing and online resource providers. Clients can now divide a single legal mandate among more than one kind of service provider to help ensure that the work is done as cost effectively as possible. Electronic storage and delivery of documents have also made the physical location of work irrelevant. The availability of online resources in virtually every area of law provides more or less equal access to the raw material of the legal profession. Legal research and document review can be conducted in any location, at any time of the day or night.

These technological advances have caused the full-service law firm model to find less favour with clients who are looking for lower-cost alternatives for more routine work. There is a willingness to 'unbundle' legal mandates and to award portions of work to whatever service provider can do it most cost effectively. The growth of legal outsourcers and other alternative service providers in recent years demonstrates that this is not simply a trend, but it is likely to be a permanent fragmentation of the legal services market. Royal Bank of Canada makes it clear in Case study 5 that outsourcing and technology are two important components of managing legal expenses.

Many law firms cannot, or may not, wish to compete with legal outsourcing companies. However, law firms must learn to collaborate with their clients to find the appropriate resources for their work, taking into account all available options both inside and outside the firm. This is most effectively done in firms with a project management capability, because it requires a breakdown of all components of a matter, as well as an understanding of the cost and availability of firm-wide resources. Project management would also facilitate a realistic assessment of the cost of various components of the work. This will make a discussion with the client of the relative value of the work much easier.

The increasing demand for alternative fee arrangements (AFAs)

The market is shifting away from hourly billing and becoming increasingly interested in AFAs. These almost always involve the transfer of some economic risk from the client to the law firm. This can obviously pose a threat to firm profitability unless these non-standard engagements can be priced and managed using some kind of project management framework. Legal project management can help a firm navigate this new pricing environment. (A detailed discussion of this is provided in Chapter 9).

The business case – Six compelling reasons

Before developing a legal project management programme for your firm or legal department, the business case must be understood by everyone involved in the effort. It helps to have a few quick responses ready for lawyers who may prefer the status quo. We have summarised the business case discussed in this chapter as follows:

- Addressing disparity – the misalignment between the way law firms work and the way clients work is not sustainable. Law is a service business that must align itself more closely with the interests of corporate clients. Project management is a structured approach that will bring a law firm's service delivery model closer to the business requirements of its clients;
- Making the link – clients want to see a clearer link between the cost of legal services and the value of those services to their business. This is more easily done within a project management framework, where the client defines what a successful outcome looks like and has a reliable estimate of the costs involved in achieving it;
- Staying competitive – the market has placed a premium on predictability, efficiency and cost control. This is not likely to change. Law firms must improve

their planning, estimating and matter management skills in order to stay competitive. Project management can do this;

- Responding to the fragmented market – clients can now divide a single legal mandate among more than one kind of service provider. Project management systems will help law firms adapt to, and perhaps even exploit, this new fragmented market;
- Responding to pricing pressures – alternative fee arrangements pose a threat to firm profitability unless they can be priced and managed using some kind of project management framework; and
- Opportunity for market differentiation – although project management is not new, the legal profession has been slow to recognise its benefits. This presents a rare opportunity for market differentiation. Law firms that are prepared to make project management a priority are in a position to have an early-mover advantage in an increasingly sophisticated and competitive market.

References

1. Susskind, R., *The End of Lawyers?* Oxford University Press, 2008.
2. 'Defining what clients want, themes from regional sessions', The ACC Value Challenge, Association of Corporate Counsel, 2008-2009.

Chapter 2: Project management foundational principles

IT IS helpful to gain a foundation in project management theory before applying the tools and techniques to a legal practice.

This chapter provides an explanation of basic project management principles and the people and processes involved in managing projects. These concepts are then incorporated into a simple legal project management framework in the following chapter. Skills, tools and techniques that support this framework are subsequently described in detail in the following chapters, with one chapter devoted to each project stage. We provide simple diagrams to illustrate the relevant components of each stage, in order to make them easier to remember and apply. We conclude Part One with a comprehensive legal project management framework, including supporting tools and techniques.

What is project management?

Project management is a structured approach to planning and managing projects. It is a recognised discipline with a standard set of skills, tools and techniques used across all industries. It began its evolution as a distinct profession in the 1950s as organisations started to systematically apply project management techniques to complex engineering projects.[1] As project managers became more experienced, a body of knowledge developed into a set of standards described in *A Guide to the Project Management Body of Knowledge (PMBOK® Guide).*[2] The legal project management framework described in this report is based to a large extent on the *PMBOK® Guide*.

There is a wide variety of recognised project management tools and techniques that have been used for decades, primarily by engineering and information technology professionals. The key to introducing project management to lawyers is to adopt only those principles that will be useful in a legal practice and, above all, to make it simple. The discussion of project management in this report focuses on those tools and techniques that are simple and useful enough to be embraced by a busy practising lawyer.

Although project management has been used with success for years in other disciplines, the complex and adversarial nature of legal work is seen to be ill-suited to a standard set of rote management processes. More fundamentally, lawyers have difficulty characterising legal matters as projects. However, we hope it will become clear in this report that principles borrowed from the field of project management can be adapted to a legal practice with great results for both law firms and their clients.

What is a project?

A project is "a temporary endeavour undertaken to create a unique result".[3] Although the end result of a project is often intended to be permanent (a building or the acquisition of a new business), the project itself has a specific beginning and end.

A legal mandate begins when a client engages a law firm to work on a matter with a view to obtaining a desired result. The mandate ends when the result is achieved or when it becomes clear that the result is not achievable. Accordingly, there is no reason why legal matters would not benefit from practices that have been developed, tested and used with success for years by professional project managers.

The Project Management Institute (PMI) is the leading international association for the project management profession. It provides numerous levels of professional certifications. PMI has recently given more attention to legal project management. In September 2010, PMI launched what is called a 'Community of Practice' or 'Virtual Community', focusing solely on legal project management. The community was launched by volunteers who had a great deal of experience or interest in this area. These volunteers formed the first executive committee for the group and are responsible for the content and operation of the site.[4]

Project management versus process management

Some law firms have looked for ways to improve efficiency in the delivery of legal services using a combination of project management and process management. The 'Seyfarth*Lean*' programme developed by Seyfarth Shaw LLP and described in Case study 4 is an adaptation of 'Lean Six Sigma', which itself is a combination of two process management methodologies. 'Six Sigma' is a rigorous methodology using data and statistical analysis to measure and improve a company's operational performance by identifying and eliminating defects in the end product of a manufacturing process. Lean is a set of principles, concepts and techniques designed for the elimination of waste in manufacturing processes. Both methodologies focus on finding the most efficient process by examining each task, asking whether it is necessary and finding the best process for performing it. Project management assumes that this analysis has already been completed and imposes a structure or discipline to ensure that each task is managed to completion.

The triple constraints

'A project can be good, fast or cheap. Pick any two.' This old project management adage captures the fundamental challenge faced by all project managers. Every project has three key constraints that must be considered together:

- Scope (good);
- Time (fast); and
- Cost (cheap).

These constraints are often depicted as a triangle (see Figure 1) to show the relationship between them and to highlight the fact that a change to one of the constraints will affect at least one – and

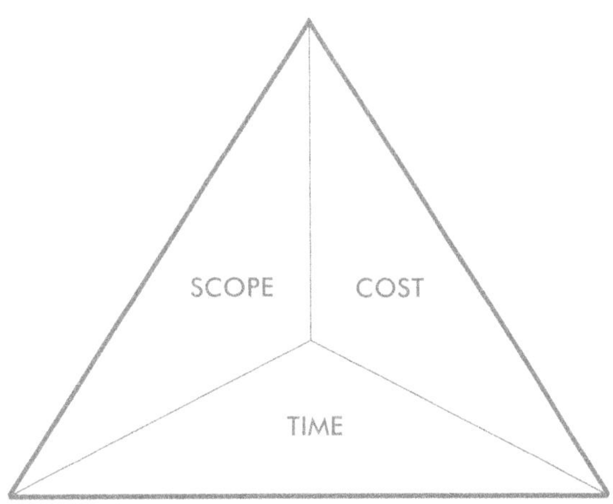

Figure 1: The 'Iron Triangle'

often both – of the other two. Figure 1 is referred to by project managers as the 'Iron Triangle'. This is a helpful model as it highlights the interdependency of the three constraints that must operate within a rigid structure. If one side of the triangle is increased, one or both of the other sides must be manipulated as well.

For example, if unanticipated work is added to a project, the scope side of the triangle will lengthen. As the scope increases, at least one other side of the triangle must move to join it. If additional resources are added to the project in order to complete the work on the same schedule, the cost side of the triangle will lengthen, but the time side of the triangle will remain the same. This is depicted further in Figure 2.

If no additional resources are added to the project, both the time and the cost sides of the triangle must increase proportionately. This is depicted in Figure 3.

The inverse of this is also true. If a client requests that anticipated costs be reduced, this cannot be accomplished without reducing the scope of the work. This may or may not affect the time it takes to complete the work.

Figure 4 depicts the scenario where both cost and time are reduced as a result of the request for a lower cost.

Clearly, there are more than three constraints in planning and managing projects. For example, if a client is prepared to accept more risk or a lower quality, these variables can be manipulated to achieve a lower cost or shorter timeline. (There are other project management triangles that depict these relationships and dependencies that are described in project management literature.) However, in a law firm, quality cannot be compromised and risks are

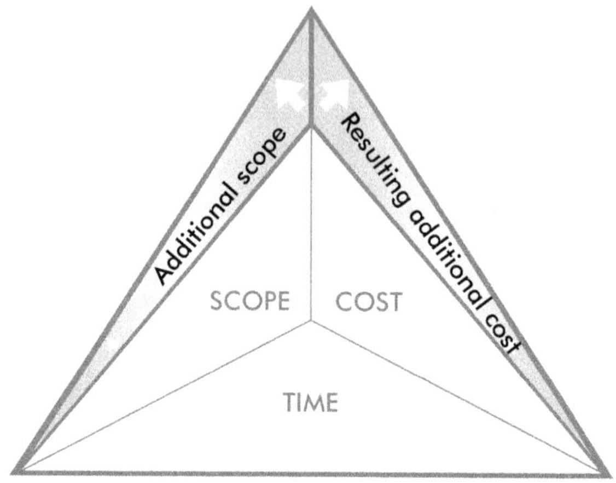

Figure 2: Increasing scope without impacting time

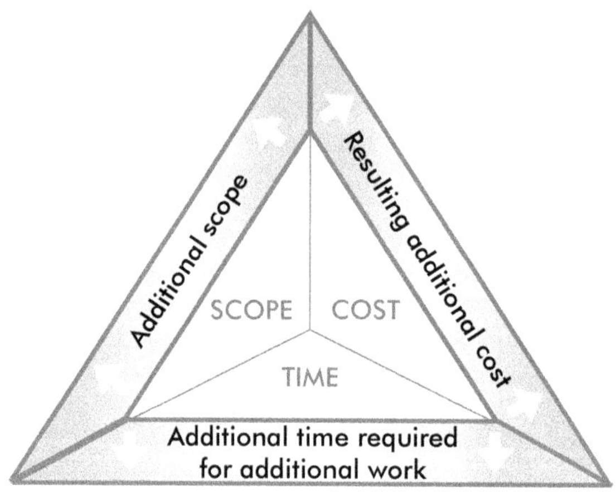

Figure 3: Consequences of adding scope

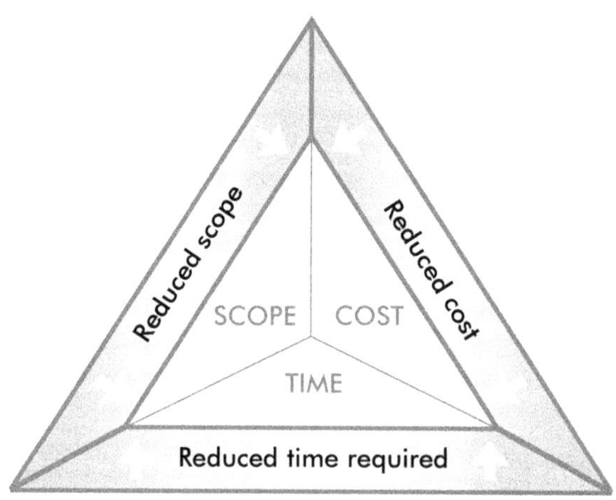

Figure 4: Consequences of reducing cost

typically assessed as substantive legal issues rather than as risks to a project's schedule or budget. In the context of a legal practice, quality and risk are not, strictly speaking, constraints that lend themselves easily to manipulation for the sake of better project management. For this reason, we focus on the triple constraints of scope, time and cost as we discuss in the legal project management framework throughout this report.

The project sponsor

A project is initiated by a project sponsor. The project sponsor is the individual employed by your client who will be leading the project, providing instructions and approving the legal fees. It is the project sponsor who has internal accountability for the project, and who must justify any cost overruns or schedule delays. After a law firm is retained on a new matter, it is of course at all times representing its client. However, in a project management model, it is sometimes useful to think of the sponsor as the individual rather than the organisation. This subtle distinction is important for lawyers to keep in mind, so as to focus not only on the legal outcome but also on the client's overall experience working with its law firm.

In a legal project management framework, 'client' and 'sponsor' are often used interchangeably. There is no harm in this. In fact, there is a benefit to reducing jargon, particularly when introducing new initiatives to lawyers. Throughout this report, we will use both terms, using 'sponsor' where it is useful to highlight the distinction between a lawyer's responsibility as legal adviser and his/her responsibility as project manager.

The project manager

The project manager is "the person assigned by the performing organization to achieve the project objectives".[5] He/she is accountable to the project sponsor for all cost overruns and schedule delays. The project manager is responsible for keeping the sponsor informed throughout the project and for resolving conflicts within the project team.

A project manager can be any member of a project team. In a legal project management framework, there could be a wide variety of individuals who qualify for this role, including non-legal support personnel. For this reason, the term 'project manager' is used generically throughout this report, although we often use it interchangeably with 'lawyer', particularly when providing examples or discussing project management responsibilities that are best performed by lawyers.

There are no typical personality types for project managers but the most successful exhibit the following traits:

- They must be pragmatic – although they need to understand the strategic vision and objectives of the project, they do not need to be visionaries. They must be able to focus on the details of the project without micro-managing the project team. They must be able to identify decisions that present a material risk to the project (which should be discussed with, and supported by, the project sponsor) and everyday decisions required to keep the project running efficiently. Good project managers understand that it is better to make a good decision quickly than a great decision too late.
- They should be good communicators – they do not need to be extroverts, but they do need to feel comfortable talking to people and working with a team and a sponsor to resolve issues. They must be confident enough to push back where appropriate; and

- They must remain objective – they should stay away from the blame game. As issues surface, effective project managers will raise options with the project sponsor and, in many cases, make a recommendation. Great project managers have mastered the art of negotiation and collaboration when working towards a compromise.

Project management processes

There are five key processes that contribute to the success of a project. These processes are used in all projects regardless of the particular profession or industry group for whom the project has been undertaken. They ensure the effective flow of work from beginning to end. The processes generally occur chronologically, so that output of one process generally becomes the input of another.[6] The five main processes are outlined in the following.

Process one – Initiation

This is the process of defining the desired project outcome to ensure the sponsor and the project manager agree on what is expected. At this stage, all objectives are articulated and the triple constraints of scope, time and cost are addressed. In a legal project management model, the lead lawyer has a significant role to play in this process.

Process two – Planning

A plan is developed to achieve the desired outcome. The plan will include the tasks and resources required to complete the tasks, as well as an estimate of the cost of completing the work. A summary of the plan will be approved by the sponsor, as part of this process.

Process three – Execution

The project team completes and delivers the work. In most project management models, the project manager's role is limited to ensuring effective communication with the sponsor and within the project team. However, in a legal project management model, the project manager may also be a key member of the team with many tasks to perform.

Process four – Monitoring and controlling

This is the process of tracking and reviewing the performance of the project and identifying areas where changes to the plan have occurred, or may be required. The project manager's role is to ensure the project is progressing on budget and on time, and that the agreed-upon work is being completed. In a legal project management model, these project management responsibilities could be performed by junior lawyers or non-legal support personnel.

Process five – Closing

The formal closing of the project involves the acceptance by the sponsor of the completed work, the documentation of lessons learned on the project and the archiving of relevant documents to be used on future projects.

The project life cycle

The five project management processes are typically performed in the same sequence on all projects, regardless of the specific work involved.[7] They are depicted in the PMI's project life cycle in Figure 5.

An understanding of the concepts depicted in this project life cycle is an important starting point for lawyers using project management for the first time. If one accepts that a successfully-managed project must move through each of the processes depicted in Figure 5, regardless of the specific work involved, it is not long

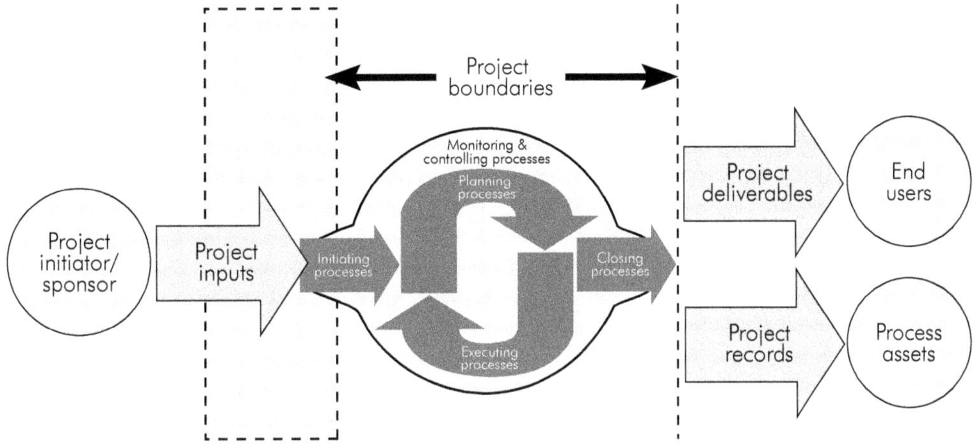

© Project Management Institute, *A Guide to the Project Management Body of Knowledge (PMBOK Guide)* – Fourth Edition, Project Management Institute, Inc., 2008

Figure 5: The PMI Project Life cycle[8]

before a model emerges that can reduce even the most complex legal mandate into its component project parts.

The project life cycle has a circular pattern. This is because unanticipated events arising during the execution process will require a return to the planning process. The monitoring process surrounds both planning and execution since it encapsulates both. This is a helpful way to visualise legal matters which, more often than not, require many deviations from the original strategy or plan.

The project boundaries that appear on either side of the circle are another key element of the model. It is critical to establish, at the beginning of a project, what is inside and what is outside these boundaries. As we will discuss in more detail in this report, unless a lawyer and client have agreed on the boundaries of the project, it will be difficult to assess whether any changes to the work are included in, or excluded from, the original fee estimate for the work.

The importance of 'process assets'

As Figure 5 shows, a completed project produces two distinct end products.

The first and most obvious are the 'deliverables', which ultimately reside with the end user (your client). In a legal matter, this could be a completed transaction or a favourable judgment.

A less obvious end product of a project is the project records – the plans, budgets, precedents and lessons learned from the processes used to complete the project. An effective legal project management model must provide a structure for saving these 'process' assets. A thorough evaluation of a project, once it has been completed, will enable the work product to be used in the planning and execution of future projects.

A few rules to live by

In addition to understanding the foundational principles upon which the legal project management framework (described in Chapter 3) is built, it helps to keep a few simple rules in mind:

- Project management is a tool box – choose only what you need to most effectively manage the project. You would not reach for a calculator to add two single digit numbers, just as it is not necessary to create a detailed project plan for a few days' work;

- Plan now or pay later – a little time upfront can save a great deal of time and effort later. While it is common to hear, 'I don't have time to create a plan, I need to get this done now', this is the equivalent of saying to a client, 'I don't have time to work efficiently, I need to do it quickly';
- The simplest process is often the best – over-complicating project management with too many processes will increase costs and reduce efficiency without adding much real value; and
- There should be no surprises – regular and effective communication is the key to successful project management. Project managers must stay several steps ahead of the sponsor of the project, who should never be surprised by anything that does not also surprise the project manager.

References

1. Elias G. Carayannis et al. (9 eds), *The story of managing projects*, Greenwood Publishing Group, 2005.
2. *A Guide to the Project Management Body of Knowledge (PMBOK® Guide)* – Fourth Edition, Project Management Institute, Inc., 2008.
3. *Ibid*, p.5.
4. For more information on PMI's work on legal project management, visit PMI's website at: http:// www.pmi.org and the legal project management website at: http:// legalpm.vc.pmi.org.
5. *A Guide to the Project Management Body of Knowledge (PMBOK® Guide)* – Fourth Edition, Project Management Institute, Inc., 2008, p.13.
6. *Ibid*, p.40.
7. *Ibid*, p.41.
8. *Ibid*, p.44

Chapter 3: A simple legal project management framework

Legal mandates are projects

In order to enhance the chances of a successful outcome, legal mandates should be managed as projects. Lawyers who lead significant matters must accept the dual responsibility of:

- Performing the legal work; and
- Managing the project.

These are two distinct roles. Lawyers have historically been experts in performing only the first role. A legal project management framework provides a context within which lawyers can perform their less familiar role as project managers.

The framework divides a legal matter into its component project parts, which are distinct from its substantive legal or procedural parts. In this framework, these are referred to as project stages, project tasks and project deliverables, in order to distinguish them from the substantive stages, tasks and deliverables of a transaction or case.

Legal mandates have four project stages

Every legal matter can be broken down into four project stages:

- Define;
- Plan;
- Monitor; and
- Evaluate.

The project manager is responsible for moving the matter through each stage.

Figure 1 illustrates the four stages of a legal project life cycle. The five project management processes discussed in Chapter 2 are depicted around the perimeter.

This legal project life cycle departs from strict project management theory in a number of ways. The 'execution' and 'monitor/control' processes have been combined into one project stage. Although these are quite separate functions that are often performed by different individuals,

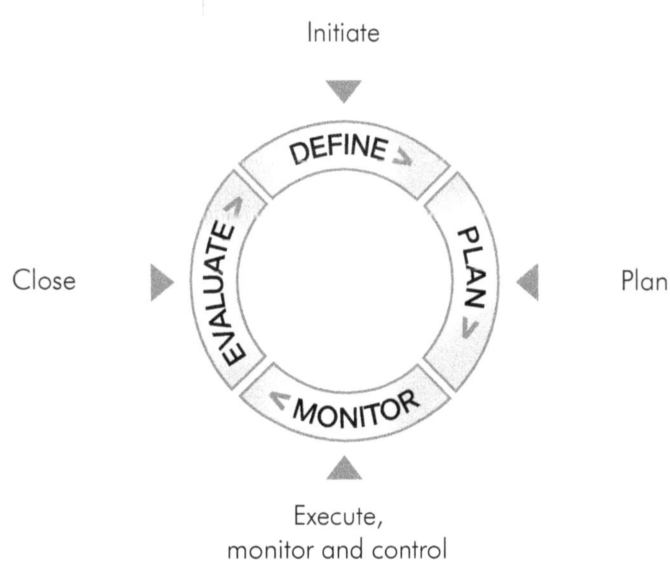

Figure 1: Legal project life cycle

they co-exist over the same period in a legal matter. In addition, the execution of legal work is second nature to lawyers and not something that requires highlighting as a distinct stage in a legal project management model.

The project stages are named with a view to emphasising those elements of project management about which lawyers, in particular, need reminding – 'Define'; 'Plan'; 'Monitor'; and 'Evaluate'.

Each project stage has two project management tasks and one project management deliverable

In order to move a legal matter through each of the four stages, a project manager must ensure that the two tasks and one deliverable that are required at each stage are completed. These tasks and deliverables are depicted in Figure 2.

From Chapter 4 to Chapter 8, the project stages are discussed in detail. Tools and techniques are provided to assist lawyers in performing the tasks and producing the deliverables required at each stage.

Your client participates at every stage of the project

One of the purposes of adopting a legal project management model is to provide law firms with the tools they need to give clients greater control over the cost and other outcomes of their legal matters. Consequently, before a project can move from one stage to the next, the client must agree with the project manager that the tasks and deliverables required at each preceding stage have been successfully completed. This requires continuous and effective communication between the

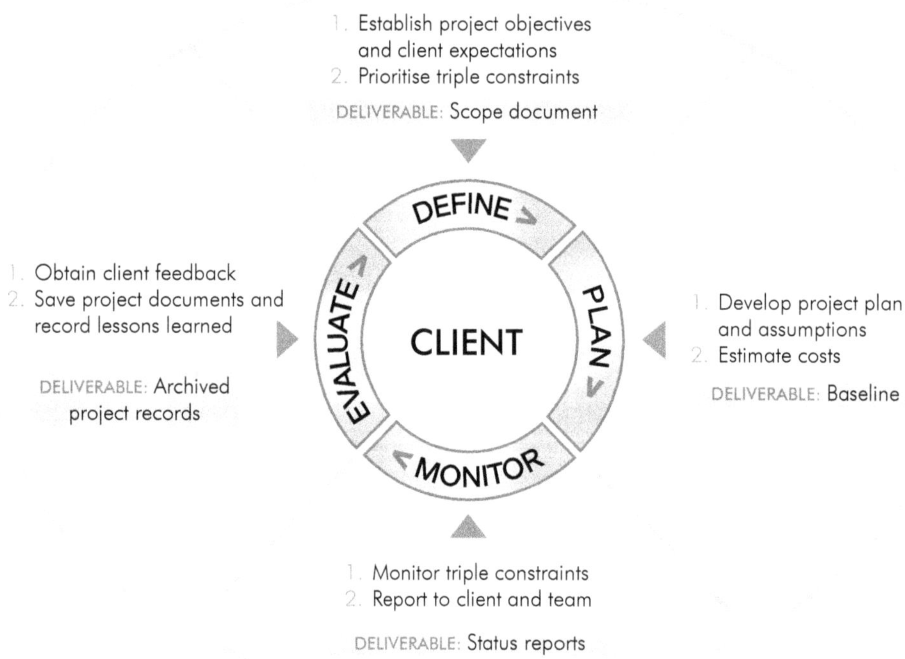

Figure 2: The legal project management framework

project manager and client at every stage. Accordingly, the client is placed in the centre of the legal project management model as shown in Figure 2.

A project manager's responsibilities can be delegated

The lead lawyer on a matter will often delegate many of his/her responsibilities to another member of the team to perform or supervise the legal work. This is encouraged for project management responsibilities as well. However, given the importance of defining clear and achievable project objectives, it is recommended that the lead lawyer perform the tasks required in the first stage of a project. All other project management tasks and deliverables can be delegated to a more junior lawyer, a non-lawyer support individual or an administrative assistant, as appropriate.

Although delegation is encouraged, the lead lawyer must remain accountable to the client organisation for the legal work product and to the sponsoring individual within that organisation for the management of the project.

Designing a framework that works

Every law firm and legal department has its own unique culture and work style. The legal project management model provided in this report was designed with the benefit of extensive trial and error, and uses tools and techniques that we believe are most relevant and useful in the practice of law. Although it should give you a head start, it will likely need to be refined or modified to work within your own organisation.

Instituting project management in a law firm is not a quick fix. It is a challenge to the status quo that requires lawyers to change the way they have traditionally worked. Resistance is inevitable and the importance of strong and consistent leadership of the initiative should not be underestimated. In Chapter 10, we provide practical advice on how to develop and implement a legal project management programme in a law firm environment.

The business case for legal project management must be made and understood by the most senior levels of firm management before any work begins. Chapter 1 provides a number of compelling business and strategic reasons to invest in legal project management. As with any internal firm initiative, support from the firm leader will be critical to its success. The development of project management must be – and must be seen to be – one of your organisation's highest priorities.

Careful consideration should be given to who will lead the initiative or, to use project management terminology, who will be the project 'sponsor'. This individual will set the objectives, timeline and budget and will have important decisions to make at every stage of the process. Accordingly, he/she should have direct access to executive authority. The project sponsor should also be someone who is well versed in firm culture and in the organisation's ability to embrace change.

You will need a project manager. Internal law firm projects involving significant non-billable commitments can be extremely difficult to manage and sustain. It will be important to choose a project manager who is able to set reasonable expectations and find ways to keep the project moving forward. The specific qualities to look for in a project manager are discussed in Chapter 2.

Finally, and most importantly, the project sponsor and project manager must firmly believe in the value of project management and be able to withstand the inevitable resistance they will encounter, so that the project can be kept on track.

Chapter 4: Defining a project

IT MAY be tempting to attribute an unsuccessful project to your client's unreasonable objectives or expectations. However, it is the lawyer's responsibility in his/her role as project manager to ensure that achievable objectives are established before work can begin.

In this chapter, the project management tasks and deliverables required in the first stage of a project are discussed. The relevant excerpt from the legal project management framework (found in Chapter 3) is reproduced in Figure 1.

Establishing project objectives

Once a lawyer accepts accountability for properly defining a project, the chances of achieving success are greatly enhanced. However, establishing and agreeing on project objectives is not a simple task. Clients may have unrealistic or competing objectives and often require the benefit of a lawyer's professional knowledge and experience to determine what is realistic in the circumstances. Occasionally, clients are reluctant to disclose their true objectives. For instance, in the case of litigation between fierce competitors in the same industry, the ultimate objectives may be much more nuanced than simply winning the case. It is a lawyer's job to elicit the true objectives of the project, so that the law firm and client can agree on what constitutes a successful outcome.

Different individuals at the client's organisation may have different or competing objectives. It is the project manager's responsibility to identify who is setting the objectives and making the decisions on the matter. It can be helpful to resort to project management terminology to distinguish between the client (client organisation) and the individual employed by the client who is leading the project (project sponsor).

For all of these reasons, we recommend that the lead lawyer perform the tasks required in the first stage of the legal project management model. The project tasks in the remaining three stages can be delegated as appropriate.

1. Establish project objectives and client expectations
2. Prioritise triple constraints

DELIVERABLE: Scope document

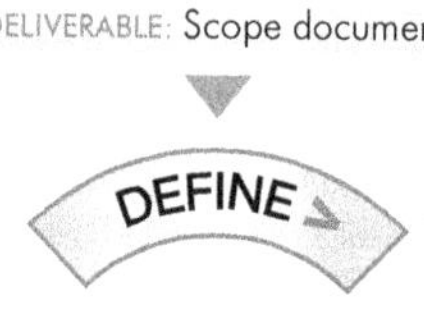

Figure 1: Requirements of the 'define' stage

A word about quality

Lawyers tend to believe that their clients' primary objective in retaining their services is to obtain legal advice of the highest quality. This is why the majority of our time and effort as lawyers is spent in the execution of a matter, focusing almost exclusively on delivering technical legal expertise. While it is undoubtedly true that clients expect our legal work to meet an extremely high standard, quality is a relative – not an absolute – concept.

Quality is defined as "the standard of something as measured against other things of a similar kind; the degree of excellence of something".[1]

To be clear, lawyers must meet high, professional standards and in this respect, the quality of legal work cannot be compromised for the sake of better project management. However, as the definition makes clear, quality is a relative measure. In a legal mandate, there will be varying levels of research and diligence required. In some cases, it may be appropriate to explore every angle. In others, a quick review or a qualified opinion is all that is needed. As long as professional standards are met, it is the project sponsor – and not the lawyer – that ultimately decides where the project should be positioned on this quality spectrum. Although professional advice may be required to enable your client to strike the appropriate balance between quality and risk, you should resist the temptation to substitute your own judgment for your client's. If you do, you will run the risk of over delivering (and over charging) without adding real value from your client's perspective.

In a legal project management context, 'quality' is best defined as meeting or exceeding your client's expectations within the specified budget and timeline. This definition should remind lawyers of the importance of the triple constraints of scope, time and cost. It reinforces the principles embedded in the 'Iron Triangle' in Figure 1, Chapter 2 – that one constraint cannot be changed without impacting one or both of the other two. It also helps lawyers remember that the project sponsor is accountable to the client organisation when matters go off course, and that the superior quality of a lawyer's work, while important, may not be his/her only concern.

Understanding and managing client expectations

Understanding that quality (for the purposes of legal project management) is defined in relation to your client's expectations, it follows that work of appropriate quality can only be delivered if these expectations are understood before the work begins. A client's expectations may be ill-formed or unspoken at the beginning of a mandate, but they will be explicit and fully formed by the end.

Consider the following example: a client has indicated that she needs an opinion on an issue of corporate governance by the end of the week. As the research is reviewed, it becomes apparent that the issue is much more complex than the client originally anticipated. The new issues are identified and analysed. The opinion takes longer than expected and the work is completed over the weekend and delivered to her first thing Monday morning. Unfortunately, the meeting of the board of directors was on Saturday, and your client expected a short memorandum on the single issue she identified, to enable her to introduce it in a preliminary fashion at the meeting. Although the work product was of a higher 'quality' than what was originally proposed and unquestionably exceeded your client's expectations, she is extremely dissatisfied with the outcome and considers the engagement to have been poorly executed.

Lawyers have a well-developed client service ethic and strive to exceed expectations. This should be encouraged as long as they are mindful of the impact this extra effort may have on the project's scope, timeline and cost. If a client has unreasonable expectations, it is the lawyer's responsibility (as project manager) to modify or otherwise manage these expectations, so that the established level of quality can be delivered.

Prioritising the triple constraints

As discussed in Chapter 2, there are three primary constraints on all projects: scope, time and cost. In the first stage of a legal mandate, it is important for both the lawyer and the client to understand and prioritise these constraints. This is not a simple exercise. Clients often start with the honest belief that all three constraints are of equal importance, however, it is the lawyer's job (as project manager) to determine the relative priority of the constraints. To use the 'Iron Triangle' illustration, the task is to find out which of scope, time and cost is the most rigid and which is the most malleable. This is the second task that must be completed before a project can be properly defined and, if done correctly, it will facilitate all of the planning, monitoring and evaluation tasks that follow. It is also important to understand that these priorities may change during the life of the project.

Consider another example: assume you have been retained by a defendant who has decided to switch lawyers three months before trial. The lawsuit is a highly-technical product liability case involving serious personal injuries. If the plaintiff is successful, the economic and reputational damage to your client's business will be substantial. The trial date has been set with no possibility of further adjournment.

The litigation is well advanced and your client has given you the files from his previous law firm. Since the case has already been worked up and there is a finite number of days until trial, your client believes that it should be reasonably simple for you to provide a fee estimate over the telephone.

You are working within the legal project management framework described in Chapter 3, so you will know that a reliable estimate cannot be provided until you have properly defined the project. You meet with your client in order to establish clear and achievable objectives, understand and set expectations, and prioritise the triple constraints.

In your initial discussion, you learn that your client's objective is to successfully defend the claim and be vindicated in the eyes of the public. He switched law firms because his previous lawyers did not, in his opinion, demonstrate the appropriate amount of advocacy experience to take a case of this significance to trial. In addition, the costs of the litigation were draining the business of much needed cash and he was looking for a lower-cost alternative.

With a fixed trial date in the very near future, time is clearly the strongest constraint. You will have no flexibility to increase the duration of the project. Cost appears to be the next strongest constraint, leaving scope as the variable most capable of being manipulated. Accordingly, you and your client agree that you will rely entirely on the work performed by the previous law firm to prepare for the trial, as a way to control costs. With the benefit of this information, you will carefully limit the scope of the project to enable your team to rely exclusively on the existing file materials.

You have also learned that your client has the competing objectives of lowering costs and providing more experienced advocacy counsel. You clearly have expectations to manage. It is your responsibility to ensure that your client understands that senior counsel charge significantly higher rates than less experienced counsel. That said, you can undertake to find the lowest-cost resource to do all but the trial advocacy work.

Active listening

In the initial client meeting, it is particularly important to keep in mind your dual role as lawyer and project manager. As a lawyer, you will be providing information in the form of professional guidance and direction. As a project manager, you will be seeking information to determine your client's objectives, expectations and the relative priority of the triple constraints.

In most cases, you will have to take the lead in eliciting this information. There are active listening techniques that you can use to increase your chances of success:

- Forced hypotheticals – one way to discover your client's true objectives is by forcing the project sponsor to consider what he/she would do when confronted with various scenarios. For example:
  - If the conditions of this transaction could not be satisfied, would you re-price the deal or walk away?
  - If you could renegotiate your credit facilities to defer interest payments, would you still go through the process of seeking concessions from your union? and
  - If an otherwise favourable economic settlement required an admission of liability, would you accept it?
- Open-ended questions – this is another technique to assist your client in defining objectives, for example:
  - How would you describe a completely successful outcome?
  - What is the worst-case scenario?
  - What issues in your business are you trying to address? and
  - What are some of the business results that you are expecting?

Let's continue with the example of the product-liability case. You intuitively believe that the solution reached with your client regarding the scope of the work may be too simplistic, given the significance of the litigation to your client's business. Before concluding the meeting, you pose a few forced hypothetical and open-ended questions, as follows:

Q: If you received a favourable settlement offer, would you accept it?
A: No. We need the public to know we are not responsible.

Q: What is the impact on your business if we lose at trial?
A: We won't lose. There is a memorandum in the previous firm's file that says that we cannot lose.

You now have a better understanding of the risks associated with relying on the previous law firm's work. A different approach to the engagement is needed. You explain the risk that your client is taking in relying on a single memorandum as the basis for the litigation and settlement strategy. You suggest that your firm spend the time and money required to review the conclusions reached by the previous firm on the probability of success. Once this 'pre-project' is concluded, you can discuss a realistic plan and strategy, and provide a revised estimate of the cost of going forward.

When you have a clear understanding of objectives, expectations and constraints, you will be able to record these in the scope document, move the project to the next stage and begin working on your project plan and fee estimate. If you do not, you will have to go back to your client and start again.

The scope document

In strict project management models, every project has a 'charter' that defines the project.

In legal project management, the concept of a charter is adopted in the form

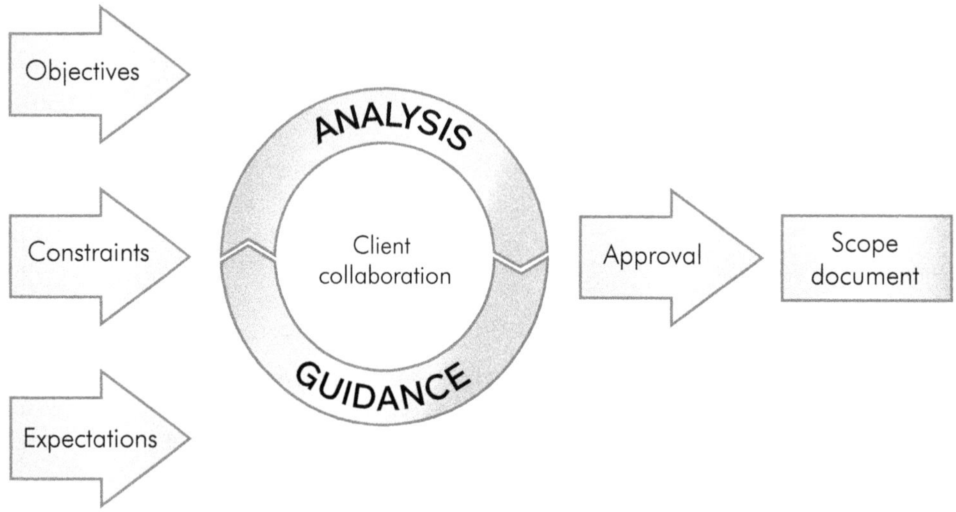

Figure 2: A project definition model

of a scope document. This is a record of what was decided in the initial conversations regarding the scope, assumptions and expected timeline. Most law firms have a standard form of engagement letter to which this scope document can be attached.

The scope document should include the following:

- Scope of work;
- Expected timeline;
- Key assumptions;
- Frequency of updates;
- Key milestones or decision points;
- Key phases; and
- Key risks that would cause the expected scope, timeline or cost to be altered, plus any mitigation strategies.

A demonstration of the importance of a scope document can be found in Case study 2 in Part Two of this report.

A project definition model

It is helpful to think of the concepts discussed in this chapter in the form of a simple illustration of the steps required to move through the first stage of a legal project. In Figure 2, the first three arrows are the project 'inputs' that will be derived from the initial meetings with the project sponsor. These inputs are analysed and discussed in order to arrive at clear and achievable project objectives. Once agreed to, these objectives are recorded in the scope document.

Reference

1. See: http://oxforddictionaries.com

Chapter 5: Planning a project

THERE IS no such thing as a perfect plan. In fact, for an experienced project manager, one third of all estimates will be high, one third will be low and the remaining third will be correct. We call this generally-accepted rule of thumb in project management estimation, the 'rule of thirds'. If experienced project managers expect only this level of accuracy in their estimates, it is no surprise that lawyers tend to be sceptical about the utility of budgets and plans.

In this chapter, we will discuss tools and techniques to help lawyers with the daunting tasks and deliverables required in the second stage of a project – the planning phase. The relevant detail from the complete project management framework provided in Figure 2, Chapter 3 is reproduced in Figure 1.

Figure 1: Requirements of the planning stage

Planning and estimating are usually the most difficult skills for lawyers to master. While there are many tools and techniques lawyers can borrow from the field of project management to improve these skills, they can be somewhat arithmetical and relatively complex. Don't be discouraged by this. Most of the mathematical formulas that are discussed in this chapter can be built into simple Excel spreadsheets and will not be apparent to the lawyers using the tools. Project planning involves each of the following components of planning a project:

- Planning tasks;
- Estimating costs;
- Recording assumptions;
- Staffing;
- Establishing a schedule;
- Establishing a baseline; and
- Addressing project risks.

A word about planning

When starting project management, many lawyers believe that creating a plan is not useful because the progression of a legal matter is beyond their control. However, a project plan is not a strict playbook; it is a path to follow. Project plans are meant to be flexible and should be updated to account for new information and circumstances. In Case study 3, Eversheds LLP describes its project plans as 'living' documents and reinforces the idea that project plans are not an attempt to predict, but rather an exercise to gather all available information, so that the current best path can be chosen.

A project manager can decide when the path should be changed and, perhaps more importantly, assess the impact of the changes on the triple constraints of scope, time and cost.

Planning tasks – The work breakdown structure

A work breakdown structure (or WBS) subdivides a project into smaller, more manageable components.[1] It is a list of all known tasks required to be completed during a matter, organised into logical groups or phases. A WBS could take many forms, including a detailed list of phases and tasks in a spreadsheet, a to-do list or a flow chart.

For legal matters, we recommend the use of a template project plan. A generic version can be found in Appendix 2. An excerpt from a completed project plan for an asset purchase transaction is provided further in this chapter.

Project plan templates can be created within law firm practice or industry groups for matters that are commonly performed by the lawyers in those groups. In developing a project plan template, it is good practice to hold brainstorming sessions with the lawyers who will ultimately be using the templates. The lawyers who will be using the templates are in the best position to create the WBS. The assumptions made when listing the tasks should be recorded in the template to ensure that they are considered at the planning stage. It is also helpful to validate project plan templates by comparing them to actual client matters of the same type.

A common dilemma when creating a project plan is deciding on the appropriate level of detail. A WBS should be detailed enough to be understood by the lawyer performing the work, but must leave enough latitude for the exercise of professional judgement. It is good practice to plan upcoming tasks at a more detailed level than more distant tasks. As a general rule, work should be broken down into tasks that are no longer than two weeks and no shorter than four hours. As with all project management principles, this is a simple guideline, not a strict rule.

Another technique used by professional project managers to create an appropriately detailed WBS is the process of progressive decomposition, i.e. start with the end deliverables and break them down into the smaller components required to achieve the end result.

DRAFT, NEGOTIATE AND FINALISE AGREEMENTS

Table 1: WBS with insufficient detail

DRAFT, NEGOTIATE AND FINALISE ESCROW AGREEMENT:
Obtain precedents
Review precedents
Review proposed agreements
Document any discrepancies
Review list of discrepancies with partner
Modify list
Contact the client to discuss comments
Obtain instructions from the client
Revise the agreement to reflect the deal and client instructions
Send to the partner for review
Send to the client to review
Obtain confirmation from the client
Send to vendor counsel
Negotiate with vendor counsel
Review comments from other side for reasonableness

Table 2: WBS with excessive detail

An insufficiently detailed WBS will lead to unreliable estimates and inefficiencies arising from misunderstandings of the required work. Excessive detail will lead to micro management and inaccurate tracking. Table 1 and Table 2 show inappropriately low and high levels of detail respectively, while Table 3 shows the recommended level of detail.

DRAFT, NEGOTIATE AND FINALISE AGREEMENTS
Escrow agreement
Non-competition agreement
Consulting agreement
Employment agreement
Transitional services agreement

Table 3: WBS with appropriate level of detail

Estimating costs – The certainty factor

Once the tasks have been identified in a WBS, the time required to complete the tasks must be estimated. This is the most difficult part of project planning for lawyers, who are quite reasonably reluctant to commit to estimates that seem no better than guesses. However, estimates do not have to be perfect and there are techniques available to improve the odds.

It is possible to assign a numerical measure of confidence known as a 'certainty factor' to the time estimated for any particular task. These are expressed as percentages with 100 per cent being the highest level of confidence in an estimate.

By assigning a numerical certainty factor to each task, you will be able to calculate a weighted average certainty factor for the entire project, which can be used to determine your overall estimate for the mandate.

Certainty factors assigned to tasks will also enable you to identify the true variables in the estimate. This will help you direct conversations with clients on the key areas of project risk (which is not necessarily the same as the legal risk). Tasks with the lowest level of certainty pose the greatest risk to the cost and schedule of the matter. Since a low certainty factor means the risk in the estimate is high, these are key areas to be discussed with your client at the outset.

In a discussion using relative levels of certainty, clients may be able to shed more light on the project itself. This may increase the certainty percentage for particular tasks and correspondingly reduce the range of the overall estimate. Alternatively, clients could decide to delay the engagement to gain more insight into the portions of the work that have a very low degree of certainty. For example, if your client is acquiring a company with potentially significant environmental liabilities, it may decide to conduct a due diligence project on this discrete issue, before incurring the cost of moving forward with the acquisition.

Certainty factor formula A

Inexperienced project managers tend to underestimate the time required to complete a task and lawyers in particular will be concerned that the actual time spent might exceed the estimate given for the work. In this situation, lawyers should choose a certainty factor formula that uses the original estimate as the lower end, as follows:

Low estimate = Estimate
High estimate = (2 – Certainty factor) x Estimate

For example, for a task with an estimate of ten hours and a certainty factor of 60 per cent, the estimate range is ten to 14 hours. This assumes that the uncertainty relates only to whether the estimate is too low.

Certainty factor formula B

On many occasions, lawyers will be pricing work in a competitive process and will not want an excessive amount of cushion built into the estimates. There is a second certainty factor formula that assumes the original estimate could be either too high or too low. This method will result in a lower overall estimate, but should still be in a reasonable range.

Low estimate =

$$\left(1 - \left(\frac{1 - \text{Certainty factor}}{2}\right)\right) \text{ x Estimate}$$

High estimate =

$$\left(1 + \left(\frac{1 - \text{Certainty factor}}{2}\right)\right) \text{ x Estimate}$$

A comparison of the different results achieved by using the two formulas on a ten-hour task with a certainty factor of 60 per cent and rate of US$400/hr is illustrated in Table 4.

	Formula A	Formula B
Hours	10 – 14	8 – 12
Cost range	US$4,000 – 5,600	US$3,200 – 4,800

Table 4: An illustration of the different results achieved using 'Formula A' and 'Formula B'

The certainty factor formulas can be applied at the phase level or overall plan level once the plan is complete. For example, an engagement with a 200-hour due diligence component could be priced using either of the methods highlighted in Table 5.

	Formula A	Formula B
Hours	200 – 250	175 – 225
Cost range	US$80,000 – 100,000	$70,000 – 90,000

Table 5: Pricing an engagement using 'Formula A' and 'Formula B'

The mathematics involved in certainty factors can be built into any Excel-based project plan template, which will make the calculations virtually invisible to lawyers using the tools.

A word about contingency

While certainty factors quantify the variability of a planned task, a contingency is used to account for the variability of unanticipated tasks that were not included in the original project plan.

In a competitive bid situation, a significant contingency amount could mean the difference between winning and losing the engagement. On the other hand, if the project sponsor requests a solid estimate and wishes to avoid going back for additional approvals, a contingency placeholder may be appropriate. Fixed or capped fee engagements should always have some sort of appropriate contingency built in.

The importance of assumptions

A critical feature of a project plan is the list of assumptions upon which the task, time and cost estimates are based.

General assumptions

General assumptions will apply to all matters of a similar nature. For example, on a simple bank financing, one might make the general assumption that the bank's standard form of loan and security documentation will be used. General assumptions of this nature can be built into the project plan template for a particular transaction and should be considered prior to starting a project plan (see, for example, the type of project plan template used by McCarthy Tétrault LLP in Case study 1).

Specific assumptions

Task or phase specific assumptions are made as the project plan is developed. For example, at the task level, in order to estimate how long it will take to prepare experts for trial, you obviously need to make an assumption about the number of experts you will need. Similarly, in order to estimate how long it will take to complete the due diligence phase of an acquisition, an assumption must be made about the number of documents to be reviewed. In the project plan template in Table 6, there is a separate column beside each task where these specific assumptions can be recorded.

The discipline of recording all assumptions will increase the chances of you and your client reaching a common understanding regarding the limitations of the estimate. A complete list of general and specific assumptions should be included with any fee estimate provided to your client. It will be an invaluable reference for managing any future surprises.

Staffing – The benefits of mindfulness

One of the basic principles of good project management is assigning the right work to the right level of professional resource. All too often, legal teams are put together without a great deal of thought or purpose. Busy lawyers tend to choose the closest, most familiar or, most available, individual without necessarily considering whether he/she is the best professional for the work. We call this 'mindless staffing' and this has a significant opportunity cost.

You may recognise some of these classic examples of mindless staffing: assigning work to the associate you like working with or to the first associate you find, or simply doing the work yourself because you are too busy to supervise someone else.

This approach to staffing is not cost effective for your client and, as we discuss in Chapter 9, can adversely impact the profitability of the matter. It does nothing for your firm's training and professional development goals, and often wastes an opportunity for future business development through the introduction of new lawyers at various levels of your client's organisation. A good example of the importance of staffing decisions is provided by Dechert LLP in Case study 2, Part Two.

A legal project management framework provides the discipline necessary to overcome this mindless staffing impulse. In our legal project management model, tasks are assigned to the appropriate level of professional resource first and the individuals who will perform the tasks are chosen later. In the recommended project plan template in Appendix 2, different levels of professional resources, from student to equity partners, are indentified. This form of project plan encourages lawyers to assign the right work to the right level, since it is only after the work has been assigned to the appropriate level of resource that the specific individuals can be chosen.

Example of a project plan

An excerpt from a project plan that incorporates many of the concepts discussed in this chapter is provided in Table 6. For illustrative purposes, we have assumed that the engagement involves the purchase of assets of a business. The full project plan can be found in Appendix 3.

Establishing a schedule – Understanding the critical path

When considering the triple constraints (scope, time and cost) in the context of an hourly engagement, time and cost are inextricably linked. It is important to understand the two different ways that project managers view time. Time is measured in terms of both effort and duration. Effort is the amount of time it takes

Continued on page 33

	Key assumptions	Certainty factor %	**Total hours (hrs)**
SUMMARY OF TIME		59%	510.0 hrs
PREPARATION FOR INITIAL INTERVIEW			
Transaction overview		80%	4.0 hrs
INITIAL INTERVIEW		80%	0.5 hrs
TERM SHEET/LETTER OF INTENT/EXPRESSION OF INTEREST			
Prepare initial draft		80%	4.9 hrs
Discuss with client and circulate new version of letter of intent to other side		80%	4.3 hrs
Meeting(s) or conference call(s) with other side to obtain comments, revise/review draft and settle letter of intent	Assume 3 calls	80%	8.8 hrs
PRELIMINARY MATTERS			
Initiate searches and obtain the written authorisation for release of information and the relevant government account numbers		80%	7.0 hrs
Consider the impact of the Investment Canada Act, Competition Act and other relevant legislation upon the transaction.		90%	4.0 hrs
DUE DILIGENCE			
Planning/providing advice in relation to the due diligence process and reviewing background materials		80%	4.0 hrs
Review legal due diligence documents for assignability and other issues	Assume 100 contracts	50%	85.0 hrs
Prepare due diligence report		70%	20.0 hrs
DRAFTING/FIRST REVIEW OF THE ASSET PURCHASE AGREEMENT (APA)			
Prepare initial draft of the APA and send to client		70%	39.0 hrs
Obtain comments and revise APA		70%	20.5 hrs
NEGOTIATE/FINALISE APA WITH OTHER SIDE			
Meeting(s) or conference call(s) with other side to obtain comments and make revisions to finalised agreement	Assume 4 meetings with other side + 2 client meetings	50%	133.0 hrs
DRAFT, NEGOTIATE AND FINALISE OTHER AGREEMENTS:			
Transitional services agreement	Bespoke agreement required	50%	16.0 hrs
Escrow agreement	Bespoke agreement required	50%	8.0 hrs
Consulting agreement	Bespoke agreement required	50%	8.0 hrs

Employment agreement	Bespoke agreement required	50%	16.0 hrs
Non-competition agreement	Bespoke agreement required	50%	8.0 hrs
PRE-CLOSING			
Prepare/review all necessary documentation		60%	57.0 hrs
Update the searches		80%	4.0 hrs
Prepare for, and conduct a pre-closing		60%	34.0 hrs
CLOSING		90%	10.0 hrs
POST-CLOSING BRIEF		80%	14.0 hrs

Table 6: An excerpt of a project plan (using an asset purchase transaction as an example)

Continued from page 31

to complete a task, i.e. the billable time recorded (for example,16 hours). Duration is the period of time over which the task is completed (eight hours per day = two days). If the principal concern is that the project be delivered on budget, greater attention should be paid to the effort which is directly related to the cost (hours x rates). However, if the project has fixed deadlines, more attention should be paid to the timeline, since the duration of the work will be as, or more important than, the effort involved.

Project managers keep projects on schedule by identifying the critical path through the project. The critical path is the sequence of activities that must be completed on schedule, in order for the project to be completed by its deadline. If any task along this path is delayed, unless appropriate actions are taken to make up for the delay, it will result in a delay in the end date of the project. The tasks identified on the critical path are not necessarily the most important, but they must be completed on time in order for the project to be completed by the deadline. As a project evolves, new tasks can become part of a redefined critical path, so it is important in a time-sensitive matter for the project manager to review the critical path regularly.

The example in Figure 2 is a simple illustration of the concept of the critical path. Assume that your firm has been engaged in the acquisition of a business and the closing is scheduled for Friday. Assume that Kate is working on the transitional services agreement, the escrow agreement and the consulting agreement while Stephen is working on the employment agreement and non-competition agreement.

In the Figure 2 example, Kate's tasks are on the critical path and are portrayed in the solid blocks. Stephen's tasks are not on the critical path because his tasks can be delayed by up to one day without changing the project's end date (Friday).

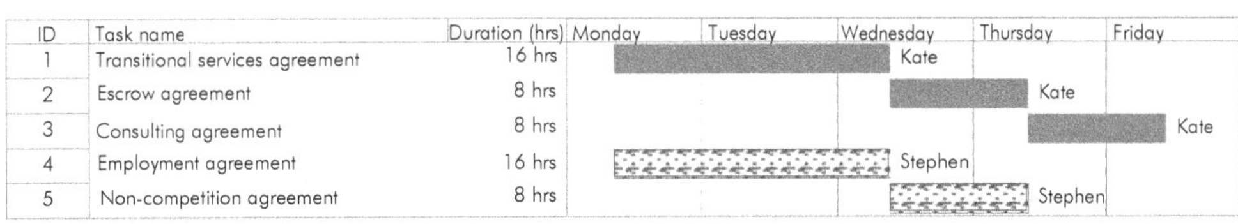

Figure 2: Determining the critical path

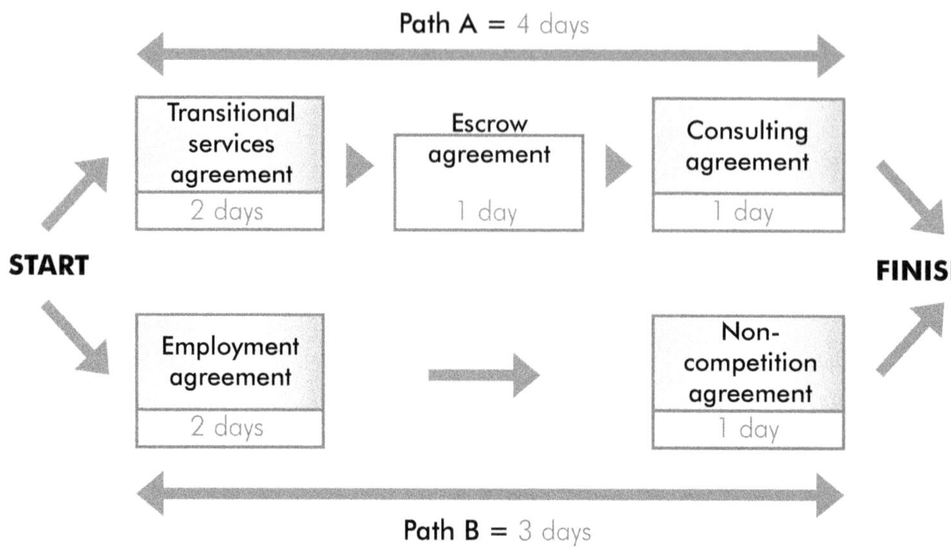

Figure 3: A network diagram showing the critical path

Both Stephen and Kate plan to start their respective tasks on Monday. Kate expects to finish her tasks on Friday while Stephen is expected to complete his tasks by Thursday. Assuming these are the only agreements left to be settled, if Stephen's agreements are delayed by one day, he will still complete them by Friday. This will have no impact on the timeline of the overall project. However, if Kate's agreements are delayed by one day, the overall project will be delayed by one day.

Of course, there will be many more tasks that will influence a timeline, making the critical path quite difficult to determine. However, it is a process that is commonly used by corporate clients in the management of projects, and lawyers should be conversant with it. Project management software tools typically have a function to highlight the baseline critical path or the current critical path, which can make the critical path assessments somewhat less onerous.

Without automated software, the critical path can be determined manually using a network diagram, as in Figure 3.

Another tool that project managers use to keep projects on track is the Gantt chart. An example of a Gantt chart is provided in Appendix 1. Designed in 1917, it is still considered to be an effective tool for managing projects. There are many software products available to create Gantt charts, from applications that can be installed on your computer (for example, 'MS Project'), to web-based tools (for example, 'Google Docs Gantt Gadget') on the internet. These charts can also be created through a spreadsheet programme such as Excel or drawn as a picture in PowerPoint.

Establishing a baseline – Discussing the plan with your client

Once you have a work breakdown structure, a staffing plan, a fee estimate and comprehensive assumptions, you have your initial project plan. Your next step is to turn the project plan into a baseline by obtaining the approval of your client. Without a proper baseline, it is impossible to understand how the project is progressing against the original plan.

While detailed planning is very useful for internal purposes, sharing a detailed plan with your client can create expectations of precision that will be difficult to meet. When considering the best way to present the project plan to your client, remember the 'rule of thirds'. Accepting that you will underestimate one third of the time, overestimate one third of the time and be correct one third of the time, you should be cautious about sharing a project plan that has been used primarily for internal planning purposes. A higher level summary is almost always preferable. We recommend that a full list of the tasks be shared but that the time and cost estimates be provided on an overall project or phase basis.

When discussing a project plan with your client, take advantage of some of the tools and techniques discussed in this chapter:

- Use certainty factors to highlight the variables in the estimate. If the range of the estimate is too wide to meet your client's planning or budgeting constraints, revisit all tasks with a certainty factor below 50 per cent and discuss whether more information is available to increase the certainty and, therefore, narrow the range of the estimate;
- Create a staffing profile – one of the benefits of a project plan template that assigns tasks to a level of resource rather than to a specific individual is that a staffing profile can be created to allow your client to see the percentage of time spent on the matter by each level of resource. A sample staffing profile is provided in Appendix 5. This will give your client an opportunity to consider the appropriateness of the overall work allocation without the necessity of providing an overly-detailed project;
- Review each task in the project plan and remove any work that your client believes will not add value. If there are tasks that can be done more cost effectively through outsourcing or by your client's own in-house legal team, agree that they are out of your scope and adjust the cost estimate accordingly. Eversheds LLP provides a good discussion of the value of this practice from both the client and law firm's perspective in Case study 3; and
- Review the assumptions with your client to ensure that they are fully understood. If you discover that an assumption is incorrect at the beginning of a matter, it is easily addressed with a revised plan and estimate. The same cannot be said for assumptions that are found to be incorrect at the end of the matter. If you have invested the time at the beginning to review all assumptions with your client, then even this unfortunate outcome is manageable.

Once the plan has been approved by your client, a permanent (read-only) version should be saved. This will become your baseline. Your project plan will be fluid as tasks are added or removed. Some tasks will be finished early while others will be delayed. The baseline allows you to compare the actual progress against the original plan and assess how well or poorly the matter is progressing when compared to the original plan and estimate. As discussed in more detail in Chapter 7, it is against this baseline that any cost and schedule variances can be assessed.

Identifying and addressing risks

Lawyers are experts at identifying and assessing legal risks and developing strategies to deal with them. This same skill set can be applied to the management of project risks – i.e. the risks that a matter will not be completed on time or on budget. In some cases, the legal risk will also present a challenge to the schedule or estimated cost of the matter. In other cases, the risk to the project may have nothing to do with the legal risks. For example, if your client is undergoing a management change, there may be a material risk that the original objectives, scope or timeline of the project may change.

By addressing the project risks in your project plan, you will be in a much better position to manage your client's expectations and deliver what was promised. Although there are tools to keep track of project risks, they are probably useful only on very large, complex or fixed price matters that involve a high degree of financial risk to your firm. In these situations, consideration should be given to recording all material project risks on a risk log, which can be basic or as detailed as you wish. Table 7 is an example of a reasonably detailed risk log.

Column A – Risk name
This is a very brief description of the risk for easy reference in communications.

Column B – Risk description
This is a more detailed description of the risk and consequences.

Column C – Impact
For a meaningful analysis of financial impact, it is often useful to measure impact in monetary terms. If that is not practical, then a qualitative measurement such as high, medium or low is sufficient

Column D – Probability
These are the odds of the risk occurring, expressed as a percentage.

Column E – Rating
The risk rating allows a comparison or ranking of the different risks on the project. If a numerical measurement was used to describe the impact, the rating can simply be expressed as the product of impact × probability. Otherwise, this can be described more simply on a high-medium-low continuum based on the classifications of probability and impact.

Column F – Management strategy
This describes the strategy for managing the risk. The four key risk management

A	B	C	D	E	F
Risk name	Risk description	Impact	Probability	Rating	Management strategy

Table 7: An example of a project risk log[2]

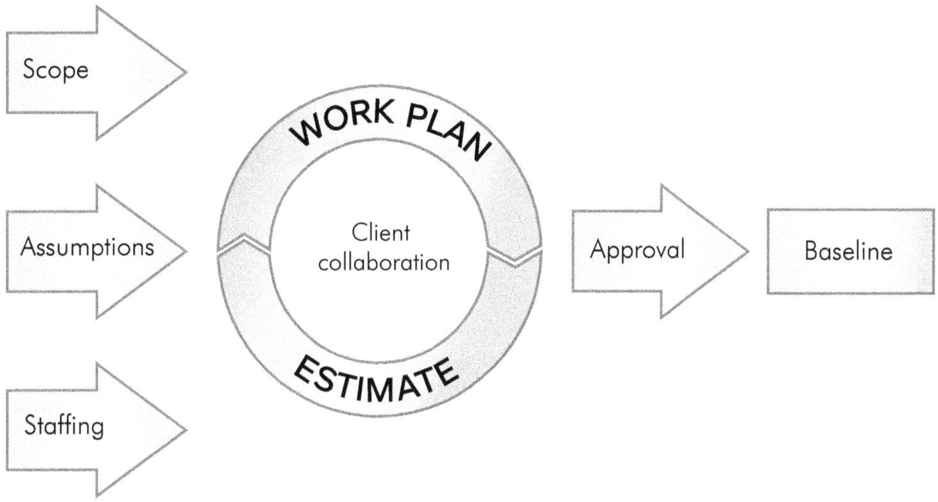

Figure 4: A planning model

strategies used by project managers (and lawyers) are:

- Mitigate;
- Avoid;
- Accept; and
- Transfer.

These can be used alone, in any combination or as alternatives.

A planning model

For ease of reference, we have illustrated the tasks and processes involved in the planning stage in the form of a model. In Figure 4, the inputs will come from the scope document created in the previous stage of the project and from your proposed staffing plan. A draft project plan and fee estimate will be developed and reworked in collaboration with your client. Once approved, it will become the baseline against which the progress of the project will be monitored.

References

1. *A Guide to the Project Management Body of Knowledge (PMBOK® Guide)* – Fourth Edition, Project Management Institute, Inc., 2008, p. 49.
2. In a risk log, there are a number of other possible columns, including identification number, date identified, category, owner, identified by, timing and last updated, to list a few.

Chapter 6: Project execution

ALTHOUGH IT may sound counterintuitive, execution is the least important process in legal project management. The actual performance of legal work is something lawyers know well and it is not necessary to build frameworks to guide them in this respect.

That said, there are a few best practices that can be employed in the execution of any project.

Project kick-off

Prior to beginning the legal work, it is imperative that the project team understand the overall objectives of the mandate, their assigned tasks, roles and responsibilities. The entire team should attend what is known as a 'kick-off' meeting. A typical agenda for a kick-off meeting is provided in Table 1.

1.	Project description and objectives
2.	Project scope overview
3.	Key assumptions
4.	Project timeline
5.	Project milestones
6.	Success criteria
7.	Project team roles and responsibilities
8.	Progress and time reporting
9.	Change control process

Table 1: A sample agenda for a project kick-off meeting

Project description and objectives

A brief overview of the mandate and its key objectives should be provided so that all members of the team have the proper context within which the work can be done. Although the objectives may seem clear to the lead lawyer/project manager, others on the team who were not involved in the initial client meetings will not have the same understanding.

Project scope overview

It is important to explain what is within the scope of the project and what is not. If there are tasks that your client has excluded but may be required as the mandate progresses, these should be identified for the team. In order to stay within the original fee estimate, it is critical for the team to focus on the in-scope work and to be able to identify any out-of-scope work that may be required, so they can inform the project manager.

Key assumptions

Sharing the key assumptions made in the planning stage will facilitate earlier detection of changes and earlier investigation of strategies to compensate for unanticipated events. It will also result in earlier communication of cost or schedule variances with your client.

Project timeline

Ensuring that everyone understands the deadlines serves to create the appropriate sense of urgency and also remind the team that other project work may be dependent on the completion of their tasks.

Project milestones

A milestone is a key event in a project. It is a useful reference point in discussions with clients who may be unconcerned with the progress of individual tasks, but will be interested in progress made towards important events. Milestones often occur at the end of a project phase. For example, in a litigation matter, the milestones could be:

- Delivery of statement of defence;
- Completion of document review;
- First day of trial; and
- Last day of trial.

Project objectives/success criteria

The key elements that comprise a successful outcome should be communicated to the entire project team at the kick-off meeting.

Keep in mind that success criteria can change over the course of the project. For example, as more information becomes available, your client may decide that the original definition of success has changed from winning the case to reaching a fair settlement.

Project team roles and responsibilities

Providing clear definitions of roles in the early stages of the project allows the team to focus on their tasks and avoid potential confusion and duplication of effort. One of the best practices for setting roles and responsibilities is to ensure these roles are put in writing before the project begins. It is also helpful to be specific about how documents and other deliverables will be reviewed, and by whom.

Table 2 is a sample list of roles and responsibilities that could be distributed at

Role	Key responsibilities
Project sponsor	■ Provide overall direction for the project; and ■ Make decisions and resolve issues.
Project manager	■ Develop, monitor and control project plan; ■ Coordinate resolution and mitigation of project issues and risks; ■ Ensure resources are appropriately assigned; ■ Manage schedules and timelines and report progress to the project sponsor; and ■ Ensure project team communication (to team leaders and the project sponsor).
Team leader	■ Build, implement, monitor and control the assigned phases of the project plan; ■ Accurately communicate progress and issues and complete status reports; ■ Attend regular project meetings to provide updates and assign/manage tasks; ■ Ensure communication/delegation within the teams; and ■ Implement action plans as required to ensure timelines are met.
Team member	■ Complete tasks assigned by either the project manager or the team leader; ■ Track time against phase and task codes on dockets; ■ Identify and resolve risks and issues; ■ Identify and obtain information required to complete assigned tasks; and ■ Adhere to project management processes.

Table 2: A sample roles and responsibilities sheet

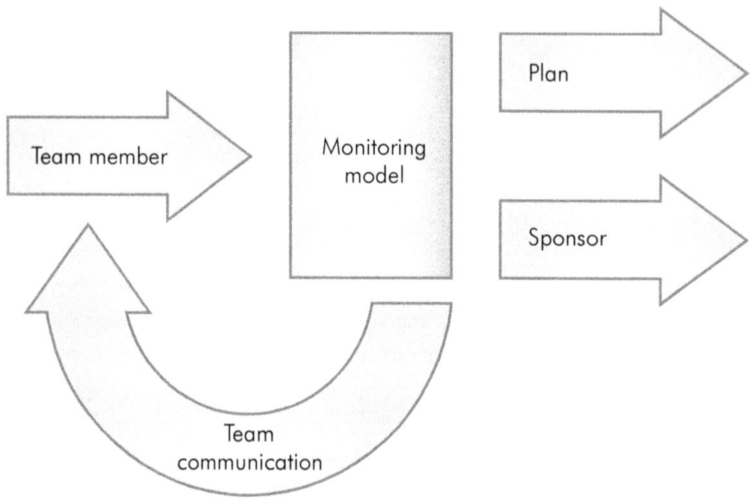

Figure 1: A team meeting model

the kick-off meeting. Depending on the size and nature of the project, you may or may not need to create many roles or provide this level of detail.

Progress and time reporting

Without diligent and accurate time recording, it will be impossible to monitor actual results against the original baseline. As the work is delivered, each member of the team must record his/her time promptly. This should be made clear at the kick-off meeting and requirements should be set for daily time entry.

Change control process

As circumstances change over the course of the matter, the project manager must be informed so that the impact can be assessed and factored into the project updates. A process for controlling these changes must be agreed on and communicated in the kick-off meeting. Change control processes are discussed in detail in the following chapter.

Subsequent team meetings

Once the project has started regular team meetings should be scheduled at common intervals to keep communication channels open and to impose additional accountability for task completion. The intervals do not need to be constant for the duration of the project as meetings may be required more often at the beginning and end of the project.

The team meeting is an opportunity to update the project manager and the rest of the team on the status of the project. By having all the team members attend one meeting rather than gathering individual updates, you will reduce matter management time and provide a forum for more effective communication within the team.

A regular team meeting agenda typically includes the following items:

- Tasks performed or completed in the previous period;
- Tasks planned for the next period;
- Key dependencies;
- Key risks;
- Key issues;
- Key decisions;
- Change orders; and
- Other concerns.

A team meeting model

The simple model in Figure 1 sets out the process for team meetings.

Chapter 7: Monitoring a project

Keeping projects on track

Projects can be monitored in different ways, ranging from highly-manual processes to fully automated systems. The tasks and deliverables required at this stage are depicted in Figure 1, taken from the complete legal project management framework provided in Chapter 3.

These are simple steps, but some of the processes behind them can be relatively complex. You will need to have:

- A baseline (discussed in Chapter 5);
- Agreed monitoring intervals (dependent on the particular project);[1]
- A system for obtaining status reports and recording time; and
- A manual or automated system for comparing actual results to the baseline.

You will also need to understand a few basic project management concepts to develop a monitoring system that works best for your firm.

Earned value

Earned value is a concept used by project managers to determine progress against a plan. It is based on the premise that the original fee estimate for an engagement is also the 'value' of that work. If the work product ultimately costs more, no value is imputed to the additional work. In the context of a legal practice, the term 'earned value' can be confusing since the price of legal work may or may not represent the real value of that work from your client's perspective. However, the concept of earned value is a cornerstone of most project management monitoring systems and is one that will be well known to clients who use project management in their own business.

As an example, if the fee estimate for a due diligence review is US$100,000 and the actual fees for the work are US$125,000, the value the client is deemed to have received is the US$100,000 that was originally estimated. In project management terms, the additional work relating to the extra US$25,000 is not seen as adding any value and is considered to be a pure cost overrun. In this situation, the project manager would determine if the overrun was caused by a change in scope, poor estimation, an incorrect assumption or other factors. Once the cause is determined, the project manager must develop a strategy for how to manage the overrun, using some of the techniques discussed later in this chapter.

Using the concept of earned value, it is possible to identify and quantify cost variances using the following formulas:

1. Monitor triple constraints
2. Report to client and team

DELIVERABLE: Status reports

Figure 1: Requirements of the monitoring stage

Earned value =

Budgeted cost of work performed x Percentage of work actually completed

Cost variance =

Earned value – Actual cost

Your client may also use a measure known as a 'Cost Performance Indicator' (CPI) to measure the overall cost efficiency of a project. The CPI provides a snapshot of the project's status at a particular point in time. The relevant formula is:

$$\text{Cost performance} = \frac{\text{Earned value}}{\text{Actual Cost}}$$

This equation produces a simple number that measures the overall cost efficiency of a project. A number greater than 1.0 indicates that the project is running over budget. A number less than 1.0 indicates that the project is under budget while a rating of 1.0 indicates that the project is on budget. These numbers can also be displayed as green, yellow or red status. An example is provided in Table 1.

CPI	Status
<0.95	Green
≥ 0.95 and ≤ 1.05	Yellow
>1.1	Red

Table1: CPI used to define budget status

The specific relationship between the CPI score and the budget status should be decided in the 'define' stage of the project.

The monitoring worksheet

There are automated systems available that can track the progress of a matter against a plan using detailed phase and task codes. Although billing codes are extremely useful when monitoring projects, persuading lawyers to use a project management model can be difficult enough without at the same time introducing mandatory billing codes on all matters. Lawyers tend to see value in the work they do, but not in the tedious task of completing phase and task codes. This might change over time as lawyers become more accustomed to using project management tools. In the meantime, we have provided

A	B	C	D	E	F	G	H
Phase / Task	Assumptions	Percentage of work completed	Budget cost	Earned value	Actual cost	Cost variance	Reason for variance

Table 2: A sample monitoring worksheet[2]

a sample manual monitoring worksheet in Table 2 that uses the earned value technique to measure progress and the following inputs.

Column A – Phase/Task
In this column, list the phase and/or task, depending on the level of detail being tracked.

Column B – Assumptions
It is helpful to list the key assumptions on the monitoring sheet to be able to identify reasons for variance.

Column C – Percentage of work completed
This is the estimate of the percentage of the work for the task/phase that has been completed.

Column D – Budget cost
For each phase/task, enter the budgeted fees for the work.

Column E – Earned value
This is the percentage of work completed (C) multiplied by budget cost (D).

Column F – Actual cost
This is the sum of the actual incurred cost of all the work done by professionals on the phase/task.

Column G – Cost variance
This is the earned value (E) minus actual cost (F). A negative number means the phase/task is over budget while a positive number indicates the task is under budget (for completed phases/tasks).

Column H – Reason for variance
A summary of the causes of the variances can be recorded here for easy reference.

An administrative assistant should be able to complete this worksheet using information available from most basic billing systems. If billing codes are not used, the information for the worksheet can be obtained by a review of timekeepers' narratives. In this event, the worksheet could be completed more efficiently if timekeepers were asked at the kick-off meeting to begin time entries with phase or task codes established for the particular matter; otherwise the same information can be obtained through status reports from team members or during team meetings.

To illustrate the mechanics of a manual monitoring worksheet, we have used excerpts from the sample project plan template in Appendix 3. We have limited our analysis to one part of the larger transaction – namely, the various employee and transitional service agreements that are common in an asset purchase deal. Tables 3 and 4 provide snapshots at two points during the transaction. Table 3 is an analysis of the status of the various agreements at a point in time following the negotiation of the term sheets, but before the agreements have been completed. Table 4 is the same analysis one week later.

At the date of the report in Table 3, the project is US$ 7,190 under budget. However, upon analysis of the data, it appears that the project was US$10,890 under budget before the report was created and that this cushion is being eroded by cost overruns in this phase.

Table 4 is a similar financial analysis of the matter one week later.

Table 4 shows that the matter is now over budget and is continuing to run off track. The project manager in this situation must determine the cause of the overrun and act accordingly. The last column in both worksheets shows that the project overrun is

A	B	C	D	E	F	G	H
Phase/Task	Assumptions	Percentage of work completed	Budget cost (US$)	Earned value (US$)	Actual cost (US$)	Cost Variance (US$)	Reason for variance
...tasks completed to settle term sheets		100%	$166,290	$166,290	$155,400	$10,890	
Escrow agreement	Bespoke agreement required	90%	$4,200	$3,780	$4,100	-$320	Agreement longer than expected
Non-competition agreement	Bespoke agreement required	75%	$4,200	$ 3,150	$4,000	-$850	Underestimated effort
Consulting agreement	Bespoke agreement required	85%	$4,200	$3,570	$6,200	-$2,630	Assumed only one agreement, but was actually three different agreements
Employment agreement	Bespoke agreement required	25%	$8,400	$2,100	$2,000	$100	
Transitional services agreement	Bespoke agreement required	0%	$8,400	$ -	$ -	$0	
...tasks after agreement negotiation		0%	$51,250	$ -	$ -	$0	
Total		72%	$246,940	$178,890	$171,700	$7,190	

Table 3: A sample completed monitoring worksheet

A	B	C	D	E	F	G	H
Phase/Task	Assumptions	Percentage of work completed	Budget cost (US$)	Earned value (US$)	Actual cost (US$)	Cost variance (US$)	Reason for variance
…tasks completed to settle term sheets		100%	$166,290	$166,290	$155,400	$10,890	
Escrow agreement	Bespoke agreement required	100%	$4,200	$4,200	$4,950	-$750	Agreement longer than expected
Non-competition agreement	Bespoke agreement required	90%	$4,200	$3,780	$5,225	-$1,445	Underestimated effort
Consulting agreement	Bespoke agreement required	100%	$4,200	$4,200	$12,800	-$8,600	Assumed only one agreement, but was actually three different agreements
Employment agreement	Bespoke agreement required	80%	$8,400	$6,720	$7,650	-$930	
Transitional services agreement	Bespoke agreement required	75%	$8,400	$6,300	$8,400	-$2,100	
…tasks after agreement negotiation		0%	$51,250	$ –	$ –	$0	
Total		78%	$246,940	$191,490	$194,425	-$2,935	

Table 4: A sample completed monitoring worksheet – one week later

due at least, in part, to a change in scope. There are three consulting agreements to be drafted instead of the one that was planned. One week earlier, when this issue first appeared, the project manager should have alerted the client to the change. At that point, the matter was still under budget and the looming cost overrun could have been addressed before the project slid further off track. Since the project was under budget just one week ago, it would be easy to assume that no adjustments were needed. However, a thorough analysis of all items in the monitoring worksheet is required in order to understand potential problems. Only then can a meaningful status report be provided to your client.

Monitoring with phase and/or task codes

The obvious advantage to an automated monitoring tool using billing codes is the availability of information for use in the current and future projects. By identifying and coding types of work, you will be able to collect data from many different projects and determine, for instance, the average time it takes to perform a coded activity on a project of a certain type. Although this information can also be obtained by reviewing timekeeper narratives, the effort involved is significant. If you are fortunate enough to have a billing system that permits the use of billing codes[3] on all matters, you will have a head start.

The adage, 'garbage in, garbage out' rings true even in the most sophisticated systems. The usefulness of an automated process depends on the accuracy of the coded time recorded. If there are confusing or ambiguous phase or task codes, or if there are simply too many of them, the resulting information may not be reliable enough to gather any meaningful historical data.

Status reports

Without phase or task-based time recording, a project manager must rely on commentary regarding the progress of assigned tasks. This can be done using status reports which typically outline:

- What each team member accomplished on the project in the previous period;
- An overview of key issues; and
- A description of the work that is planned for the following period.

Status reports can be provided verbally, in writing or at team meetings, and can provide motivation for individual team members to keep their part of the project on track.

Status reports are also provided to clients at established intervals. These are a required deliverable before the project can move to the final stage and be closed. Monitoring worksheets such as the one provided in Table 2 can be used together with team updates to prepare status reports for clients.

Managing change requests

When a project plan is first completed, it is based on information that is available at the time. As the project progresses, more information will become available which may result in changes to the tasks or the scope of the matter. The need for a change may be apparent to your client or your team, or both. In any event, some sort of change to the original plan is inevitable and it must be managed carefully.

A formal process is only necessary for changes that will have a material impact on the triple constraints of scope, time or cost. Although professional project managers typically use written change orders for any new or revised work, in a law firm environment, something less formal should be considered. A change request could be made verbally, in an e-mail or a letter.

A change control process should achieve the following:

- Confirm the change to the project plan is, in fact, required;
- Understand and define its impact on the project; and
- Ensure the appropriate individuals are informed of the change.

Figure 2 is a flowchart depicting the required steps. For more complex projects, a written change request form is provided in Appendix 6.

Addressing cost variances

Addressing cost variances is an art, not a science. Experience will help a project manager decide when a cost variance is material and when it is not. In the meantime, there are some project management techniques that can help.

As illustrated in Tables 3 and 4, a project manager must understand both the current state of the project and its history, in order to identify relevant trends. For example, if the project is currently 20 per cent over budget, because each phase was consistently 20 per cent over the expected cost, the project will end 20 per cent over budget. However, if the project is otherwise on track and only one phase is 60 per cent over budget, the issue may be limited to an unexpected protracted negotiation and may not be indicative of a systemic problem in the project.

It is common for any project manager to assume that they can make up cost variances later in the mandate. This strategy rarely pays off. Throughout the life of a project, the project manager should pay close attention to the planned and actual costs of each phase. If the first phase of the project is over the planned budget, unless the overage can be explained by the early completion of work scheduled for a future phase, this cost overrun will likely exist at the end of the mandate as well.

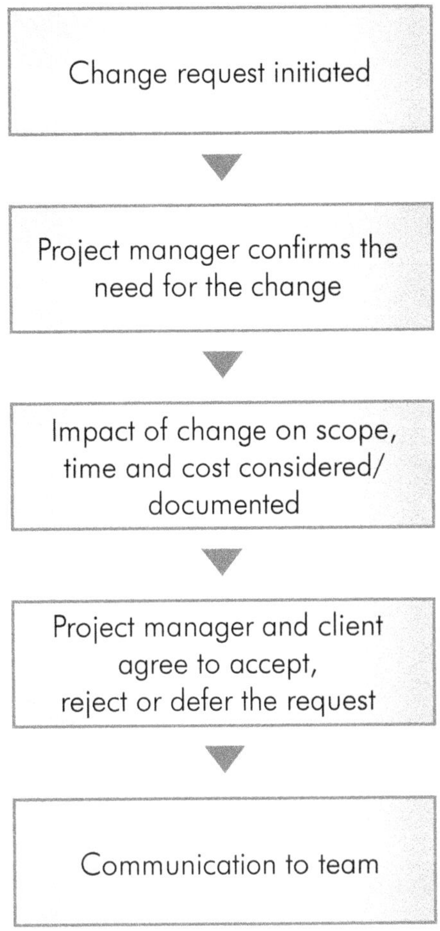

Figure 2: A change control process

The following options should be considered to best address a cost overrun:

- Reducing scope – consider whether non-mandatory work can be eliminated with the approval of the project sponsor after the appropriate risk analysis. In some cases, your client may be able to take on some of the work internally;
- Change request – if the cost overrun was caused by work that was not

planned, but was seen as valuable by your client, a change request could be made to increase the budget for the project. Where possible, change requests should be made prior to performing the additional work;

- Re-aligning resources – some work could be moved to lower cost professionals to reduce overall costs, however, there may be a quality trade-off that should be carefully considered. If the matter was staffed efficiently to begin with, there may not be much room to exercise this option; and
- Outsourcing – rather than re-aligning the resources within the team, there may be a lower-cost service provider that is able to perform some of the work.

If none of these options is available, and particularly if the overrun is the result of incorrect estimates, poor project management or turnover on the team, a law firm may be left with no option but to write off the additional fees.

Addressing schedule variances

Schedule variances are typically measured at the cumulative task level, rather than at the specific phase or overall project level. Although not intuitive, a schedule variance is measured in currency rather than time, and is calculated using the following formulas:

Planned value =
Planned percentage complete x Budget cost

Earned value =
Actual percentage complete x Budget cost

Schedule variance =
Earned value – Planned value

A negative value means the project is behind schedule and a positive value means the project is ahead of schedule. For example: assume a project with a budget of US$100,000 began on 1 January and it is now 1 March. Fifty per cent of the work has been completed, but the project plan indicated that 70 per cent of the work should have been completed by this time.

Earned value =	US$50,000
Planned value =	US$70,000
Schedule variance =	-US$20,000

Surprisingly, schedule variances can be harder to address than cost variances. If all else fails, cost variances can be addressed by clients paying the additional fees or law firms absorbing the extra cost. The same cannot be said for variances in schedule. However, there are some techniques that can help lawyers make up for delays:

- Add more resources – this will address the timeline issues but will also increase the overall cost. It may also add new costs related to duplication of effort or the additional supervision time required when bringing someone new up to speed;
- Balance resources – while some team members on the project may be behind schedule, those who are ahead can shift their focus to tasks that are on the critical path. While there is still a risk of duplication of effort, it should require less supervisory time to bring existing team members up to speed than bringing in a new lawyer;
- Fast-tracking – this is a well-known project management technique in which phases or tasks normally completed in sequence are changed to allow them to be completed in parallel. In situations where one task is dependent on the outcome of another, assumptions can be made about those outcomes to enable work to be

done on parallel tracks. There is a risk that these assumptions are incorrect resulting in unnecessary work and further delay;

- Crashing – this is a project management term for spending more money on a project that is behind schedule, knowing it is not the most efficient solution. It can include paying additional fees or premiums for priority services from agents, process servers, corporate search firms and couriers; and
- Reducing scope – in some cases, non-mandatory work can be eliminated with the approval of the client after the appropriate risk analysis.

Managing client expectations

Whatever method is chosen to adjust forcost overruns or schedule variances, your client should be informed of any consequential changes to the project plan and fee estimate. There is a fine line between burdening your client with unnecessary details and providing enough information to manage expectations. The project manager will need to exercise his/her own judgement to make these decisions.

As we discussed in Chapter 2, there should be no surprises. If you are confident that you can manage the situation so that the cost or schedule variance does not impact the project plan in a material way, it may not be necessary to inform your client. However, when in doubt, it is best to air on the side of transparency, because:

- The project sponsor will have internal accountability for cost and schedule variances and may have a preferred strategy to respond to the situation that will minimise repercussions internally;
- Involving the project sponsor in these decisions will give him/her a sense of control over the cost and other outcomes of the mandate;
- By engaging in a discussion of the options with the project sponsor, you will increase the chances that any additional cost will be approved; and
- It provides an opportunity to confirm that the triple constraints have been prioritised appropriately, which will help with any future course corrections.

Clearly, your approach will depend on the cause of the variance. For instance, if the project was properly defined and the variance is the result of an unanticipated change that increased the scope of the work, your discussion should be fairly straightforward, provided it happens as soon you become aware of the situation. However, if the matter has been poorly defined, the same circumstances may lead to a write-down of the cost overrun or, in the case of a schedule variance, the addition of extra resources at the law firm's expense.

Providing frequent and candid updates is always the best approach. Admitting mistakes often increases trust and strengthens the client relationship. In fact, honest and effective communication can sometimes compensate for poor project management. A good example of this is also provided by Royal Bank of Canada in Case study 5.

Many lawyers deal with cost overruns by making financial concessions after the bill is presented and only if their client complains. This impacts the profitability of the matter and rarely compensates for the client's dissatisfaction. In Case study 5, Royal Bank of Canada provides a client's perspective on the perils of this approach.

The monitoring model

Finally, the mechanics of monitoring a project can be illustrated in a model as shown in Figure 3.

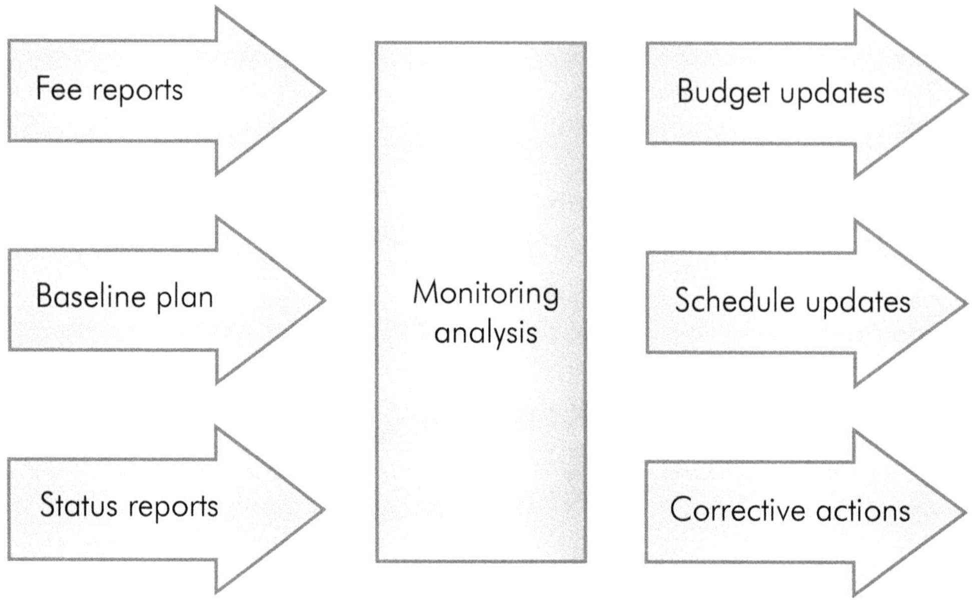

Figure 3: The monitoring model

References

1. The determination of the appropriate intervals for monitoring the triple constraints will depend on the project. There is no set standard. In a project where all lawyers are billing a total of 25 hours per week, it might be sufficient to review the progress bi-weekly or monthly. A project where several hundred hours are being billed weekly will likely require progress to be monitored weekly.
2. Note that there is no account of fees by timekeeper in this monitoring worksheet. While this level of detail is useful, it is likely to be too time consuming for a manual tracking system. Automated systems can do this fairly easily.
3. Examples of specific task coding standards include LEDES™ (Legal Electronic Data Exchange Standard)/UTBMS (Uniform Task Based Management System).

Chapter 8: Evaluating a project

Leveraging your work product

Time invested in evaluating a project and archiving useful documents and information will enable firms to gain institutional knowledge that can be used when planning, pricing and managing the next project. This is one of the most valuable aspects of project management for a law firm.

Completion of the tasks and deliverables in the final stage of a project shown in Figure 1 will allow a law firm to create a historical database of information for use on future projects.

Exploiting process assets

When working within a legal project management framework, the processes used to manage the project generate valuable records and other information that law firms can use on future matters. As discussed in Chapter 2, these are known as 'process assets'. They include tangible work products such as scope documents, project plans and fee estimates, as well as more intangible knowledge gained from feedback on the project.

While lawyers are adept at closing matters and sending the final invoice, they typically do not spend the time required to look back on the project and consolidate these process assets. Although most firms and many large in-house law groups have knowledge management lawyers who are responsible for gathering and preserving this type of information, they cannot (on their own) have the same insight into a transaction or case as the lawyers who performed the work. By ensuring that a proper evaluation of the project is conducted while memories are still fresh, law firms will be in a position to exploit the valuable process assets that are most accessible in the project's final stage.

Figure 1: Requirements of the evaluate and close stage

Obtaining client feedback

Although client satisfaction surveys are commonly used by law firms, they are typically held on an annual basis and focus on broad relationship issues. They are often conducted with the general counsel, who may or may not, have been personally involved in the specific matters performed that year. These annual interviews are extremely important client relationship tools, but are less effective for gathering feedback on specific projects. A better practice is to meet with the project sponsor as soon as the substantive work is done to obtain an evaluation of the firm's performance on the engagement. In order to highlight the need for this sort of specific, project-related feedback, it is one of the two tasks to be performed before a legal matter can be closed.

A client feedback interview can include both qualitative and quantitative measures. Generally, qualitative feedback is obtained through open-ended questions on what was done well and what could have been done better. These questions are best asked in an interview. Quantitative feedback is used for comparison purposes and sometimes form part of a law firm's internal performance reviews. These questions are best suited to a questionnaire using a simple scoring of '1' (poor) to '5' (outstanding).These two techniques can be combined by first leaving the quantitative questionnaire with the client and then following up with an interview to gather additional feedback. The follow-up interview can also be a good business development opportunity. Possible topics to include in a client satisfaction review are listed in Table 1.

The final stage of a project is also the optimal time to conduct short, specific performance reviews of the individual members of the team.

Saving project documents

By evaluating and saving project documents, law firms can leverage their work product so that future matters can be planned more

Client satisfaction review questionnaire	In person meeting	Questionnaire
1. Did the project meet your expectations?	✓	✓
a. Project successes	✓	
b. Project shortcomings	✓	
2. What worked well?	✓	
3. What did not work well?	✓	
4. Rate the quality of the work	✓	✓
5. Did the staffing profile meet your needs?	✓	✓
6. Was the level of involvement by senior partners sufficient?	✓	✓
7. Was the project delivered on time?	✓	✓
8. Was the work within the expected budget?	✓	✓
9. Communications	✓	✓
a. Cost/budget updates	✓	✓
b. Progress updates	✓	✓
c. Issue updates	✓	✓
10. Teamwork between law firm team and client team	✓	✓
11. What should be changed on the next project?	✓	
12. Overall service received	✓	✓

Table 1: A client satisfaction review questionnaire

easily, priced more accurately, managed more efficiently and performed at a lower cost. A proper evaluation of these documents can also improve your project management tools and processes, in general, for the benefit of all lawyers in the firm.

At the end of every major mandate, each of the following should be undertaken:

- Assess the finished project plan and add to the generic template any tasks or assumptions that were overlooked;
- Save all planning, pricing and monitoring records into your firm's knowledge management systems according to the type of work performed;
- Identify all documents, pleadings or agreements that will be useful substantive precedents and consider what checklists, agendas, spreadsheets and other project management tools can be added to your firm's standard templates; and
- Look for any project management forms or processes that worked particularly well and create a generic template or system for use on the next matter.

Historical data should be retrievable by searching a variety of identifiers. Keep in mind that this information can be used not only on the next matter of the same type, but also on the next project for the same client, the next case before the same judge, or the next transaction with the same opposing counsel.

The lessons learned meeting

Once the project has been evaluated by the project sponsor, the team should meet one last time to discuss the circumstances of the project and what contributed to its successes and failures. Client feedback should be shared with the team as part of the discussion. It should be very clear to the participants that the goal is not to lay blame, but to gain individual and institutional knowledge. This is called a 'lessons learned' session. The outcome of this session will be an important asset of the project. A discussion of the importance of a lessons learned meeting can be found in Case study 2.

These sessions are most effective when facilitated by someone who was not directly involved in the project. Knowledge management lawyers are obvious choices for this role. They can be objective and, since their participation at the meeting will give them insight into the project, that will enhance their ability to gather the relevant information for future use. The facilitator should guide the discussion and record suggestions, ideally in the form of a flipchart.

The meeting should strike a balance between positive feedback and candid analysis. Any comments about the performance of a specific team member should be omitted from the lessons learned document and used instead in individual performance reviews.

Table 2 is an example of an agenda for a lessons learned session.

1. Recap of project objectives
2. Overall project success
3. Project timeline – plan and actual
4. Project challenges and issues
5. What worked well and should be continued
6. What did not work and what should be improved
7. Institutional recommendations
8. Personal learning

Table 2: An example of an agenda for a lessons learned session

Recap of project objectives
The team should be reminded of the project objectives so they can compare what was originally required with what was ultimately delivered.

Overall project success
Before delving into the details of the project, allow team members to discuss their successes. This will start the meeting on a positive note and encourage them to participate and share ideas.

Project timeline
Compare the baseline plan to the actual result and note material cost and schedule variances. This will allow the team to formulate ideas for the remainder of the session.

Project challenges and issues
The team should discuss the project's key challenges, including material cost and schedule variances. Be prepared for differing opinions on the underlying causes of the issues and record ideas on a flipchart.

What worked well and should be continued
After discussing challenges, it helps to move the discussion back to positive elements of the project.

What did not work and what should be improved
After identifying problems, allow the team to engage in brainstorming to find alternatives that may have worked better.

Institutional recommendations
Summarise the findings into best practices and re-introduce them into any internal documentation and training. This will help other professionals within the organisation deal with similar projects.

Personal learning
In keeping with the spirit of positivity encouragement, have each team member share what they learned and what they would do differently. This helps end the session on a positive note.

The evaluation model
The opportunities presented by a proper project evaluation are often overlooked by lawyers but rarely overlooked by project managers. With the dual responsibilities imposed by a legal project management model and the discipline of moving through the project stages, a law firm will be better positioned to gain and exploit valuable institutional knowledge.

Figure 2 is a simple evaluation model.

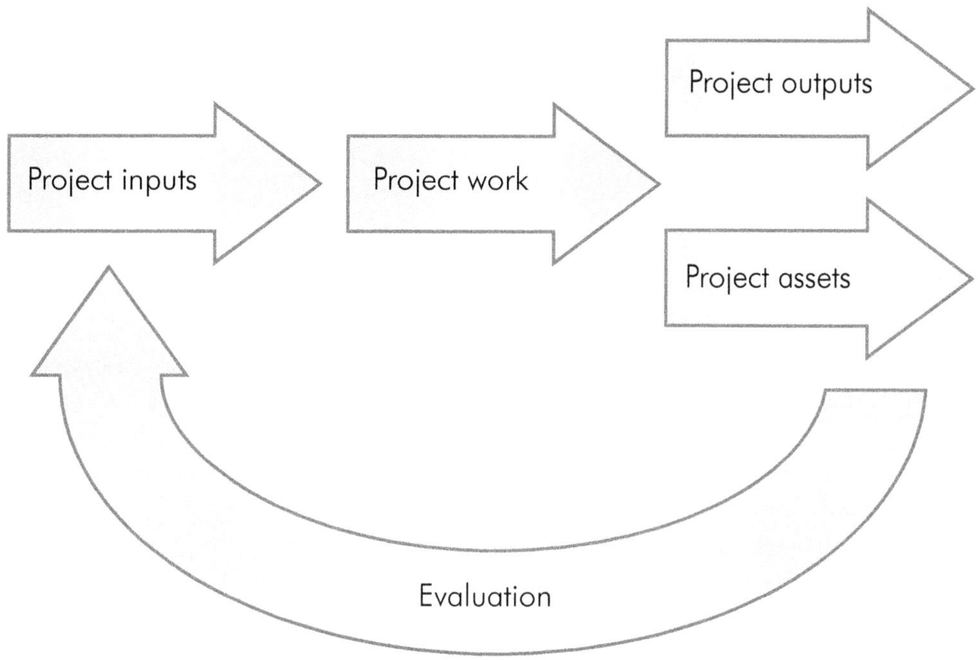

Figure 2: An evaluation model

Chapter 9: Linking project management to pricing strategies

THE COMBINATION of significant increases in law firm costs and the downward pressure on hourly rates has forced law firms to re-examine their approach to managing profitability. In the current environment, law firms must focus much more carefully on pricing the work they do and look for ways to provide the same level of service to clients at a lower cost to the firm. They must also pay particular attention to profitability on a matter by matter basis, rather than simply multiplying rates by hours in an annual budgeting exercise.

In this chapter, we discuss how legal project management can contribute to matter profitability and help law firms manage some of the more common alternative fee arrangements (AFAs).

Basic practice economics

One of the benefits of a legal project management framework is that it encourages lawyers to be mindful of the factors that influence profitability when planning, pricing and managing matters.

Figure 1 is a simple illustration of the positive and negative factors affecting law firm profitability.

It is useful to look at the interplay between legal project management and some of the positive and negative profitability drivers in a law firm.

Leverage

The staffing techniques described in this report help ensure that a matter is properly

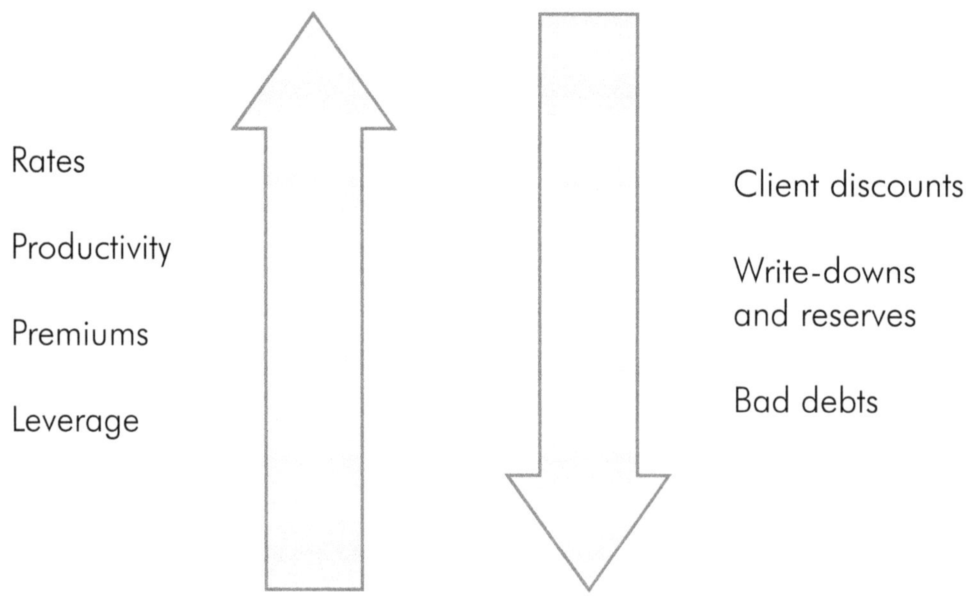

Figure 1: Variables that impact profitability

leveraged, allowing the firm to earn more profit per hour worked. Since equity partners share profits of the firm, their compensation is normally far greater than that of non-equity partners and associates, and the rate differential is typically not sufficient to compensate for this. Consequently, lawyers with the highest billable rates will typically be doing work at a higher cost to the firm.

Consider the comparative return on investment (ROI) for a senior partner and a junior associate, assuming both are producing the same number of billable hours per year, as illustrated in Table 1.

Rates

In a given year, lawyers will take on work of varying levels of difficulty and importance to clients, but will typically charge the same hourly rate on each engagement. This is a missed opportunity. It means that clients are paying too much for some matters and not enough for others. There are many instances where it may be appropriate to increase the set hourly rates of your leading experts to coincide with the importance and risk of a particular matter. By going through the discipline of properly defining the matter in the first stage of a project, you will discover whether cost is a relatively weak or relatively strong constraint and be in a position to set rates accordingly. In setting rates on a matter by matter basis, you may have an opportunity to increase matter profitability while at the same time meeting your clients' objectives.

Discounts

Since hourly billing is still the prevalent pricing model for legal services, law firms commonly respond to price pressure by offering discounted rates. This allows firms to continue to manage matters as hourly engagements, but it can materially reduce profit margins. Premiums over hourly rates are rare and typically do not offset these discounts. Legal project management offers an alternative to discounts by providing clients with a structure for more reliable estimates and more predictable outcomes. Clients may be more comfortable accepting your firm's full hourly rates if they have some degree of certainty about the total number of hours required, and some measure of control over the management of the matter.

Write-downs and bad debts

If the proper change control process is followed for unexpected adjustments to scope, schedule or cost, there should be no surprises when the final invoice is received, even if it is higher than originally agreed.

	Partner	Junior associate
Compensation	US$1,000,000	US$150,000
Overhead	US$300,000	US$250,000
Total cost	US$1,300,000	US$400,000
Billable rate	US$ 800 /hr	US$ 400 /hr
Billable hours	1,800	1,800
Revenue	US$1,440,000	US$720,000
Net profit	US$ 140,000	US$320,000
ROI	11%	80%

Table 1: ROI comparison of a partner *versus* associate

The necessity for prompt and accurate time recording will ensure that interim invoices are complete and can be sent as soon as the work for the billing period is performed. In this way, a well-managed matter should reduce the likelihood of write-downs and bad debts.

Maximise profitability through efficiency and leverage

Law firm profits are typically measured in relation to an annual budget. Revenue is estimated using assumptions about rates, realisation and billable hours. Any budgeted increase in costs for the year is typically absorbed by corresponding rate increases. As long as clients are prepared to accept hourly billing and increased rates, there is no pressing need for law firms to reduce costs to maintain profitability. However, as outlined in detail in Chapter 1, the market is challenging this business model and law firms must now find ways to improve efficiency and predictability in their matter management and pricing. There are a number of ways that a legal project management framework can help and these are discussed further.

Use data from previous projects

As discussed in the previous chapter, there are many potential best practices for increasing efficiencies and reducing firm costs that can be identified if the projects have been properly evaluated.

Calculate averages

By analysing historical information, you should be able to determine the average number of hours required to complete various types of work and make this a starting point in any future project plan. You should also be able to determine the range of seniority of professionals used on previous matters and identify the lowest-cost resource that is able to perform the required work. You can then develop standard staffing models for particular types of work that will produce an acceptable profit margin while delivering the quality that is expected by the client.

Choose resources wisely

There is obviously a wide variation in the amount of time it will take lawyers at different levels of seniority to complete the same task. Be mindful of the economics of this. Consider how staffing choices influence both the cost of the work to the firm and the price of the work to the client. Remember the differential ROI illustrated in Table 1 when allocating work between different levels of resources. Compare the amount of effort required by lawyers of differing levels of seniority and determine which combinations are most advantageous from a profitability perspective. If the work satisfies the agreed level of quality and price, your client should be reasonably indifferent as to how the work gets done. For example, assume that a simple indemnification agreement is required as part of a larger transaction that is scheduled to close in two days. The senior partner in charge of the transaction drafts the agreement, having concluded that the junior associate on the team would have taken twice as long to complete the task. Table 2 demonstrates the impact of this staffing choice.

In both cases, the client is billed US$1,600 for the indemnification agreement. However, the net profit earned by the firm is materially different. Assigning the work to the junior associate would have resulted in a higher profit margin with no impact on the price of the work to the client. The senior partner who drafted the agreement herself because she was 'too busy' to delegate the work, has cost the

	Senior partner	Junior associate
Hourly rate	US$800/hr	US$400/hr
Cost per hour (compensation + overhead)	US$722/hr	US$222/hr
Effort to perform work	2 hours	4 hours
Billing to client	US$1,600	US$1,600
Cost to the firm	US$1,444	US$888
Net profit	US$156	US$712

Table 2: The impact of leverage on matter profitability

firm US$556 in lost profits and missed the opportunity to spend two hours developing new business for the firm. The junior associate also missed the opportunity to improve his drafting skills.

Managing AFAs

As the market shifts further away from hourly billing in favour of fixed fees or strict budgets, law firms must learn how to provide an overall price that bears some relation to the value of the work to the client, while still making a profit on the matter. A discussion of Royal Bank of Canada's preference for, and experience with, a variety of pricing models can be found in Case study 5. Law firms must also develop strategies to mitigate the risks that they are now being asked to bear in the event that fees exceed the agreed amount.

The legal project management framework, tools and techniques discussed in this report can help in the ways discussed further.

Historical financial information

Historical financial information from previous engagements of the same type should be referred to as a matter of course before providing any fee arrangement where the firm is assuming a price risk. This should become a standard process for any firm considering AFAs. With sufficient historical data, your pricing conversations will be easier. You will be able to provide worst and best case scenarios on the length of time and range of fees for work that your firm engages in regularly. Eversheds believes that this is the most valuable result of legal project management and provides examples in Case study 3.

Generating profit for the firm

When analysing historical information, the key question is not whether the previous matters were performed within the agreed budget or fee cap, but whether matters that were performed according to plan generated a profit for the firm. Engagements that cannot generate an acceptable level of profit, even with the benefit of good project management, should be examined very carefully. Can they be priced or staffed differently to meet expected profit margins? If not, the firm should likely not accept work of this type in the future, unless there are other strategic reasons to do so.

Changes in the project plan

Where prior matters were profitable, consider what has changed since the matters were completed. Be sure to factor in any increases in rates and overhead, and any relevant changes in personnel.

Record assumptions

Using the project plan template described in Chapter 5 (samples of which are provided in Appendix 2 and Appendix 3), record specific assumptions next to the description of the work. Include a list of these assumptions with any fixed price proposal or fee cap. These assumptions will enable you to clearly define the parameters of the price risk you have agreed to take on and will mitigate this risk.

Taking into account management time and experience when pricing

In determining the price of a fixed fee engagement, do not overlook the time spent by the project manager and those to whom the project management responsibilities will be delegated. Once your lawyers become experienced project managers, these hours add value and are often properly chargeable. You may allocate the additional time among the various team members to whom the project management responsibilities have been assigned. Alternatively, an overall estimate of project management time could be calculated as a percentage of the final estimate and added to the price as a flat fee.

Justifying the price

If the objectives, constraints and expectations have been properly defined using the techniques discussed in Chapter 4, you will be in a much better position to determine and subsequently justify a proposed overall price for the work. You will know whether your client considers the matter business critical and you will know the relative priority of the scope, time and cost constraints. If the matter is highly specialised, very time sensitive or critical to the continuing financial strength of the business, it will obviously command a higher price.

Find other ways to add value

Focus on the project objectives that have been defined at the outset and determine if there are ways to add value to the project without adding additional costs. Would it assist your client in achieving their objectives if one of the team members (who might otherwise be under utilised) were seconded to the client for the duration of the project? Could the firm conduct a legal education seminar on a topic of relevance to the project and invite the client's project team?

Cost variances

Cost variances will be a key concern for the firm and the reason for the variance must be determined promptly. Fixed fee arrangements can be managed using the monitoring processes described in Chapter 7. It is a good practice to increase the number of monitoring intervals for internal purposes and to consult the scope document, baseline and the relevant assumptions at each interval, to confirm that all work is in scope and that any out-of-scope work or changed assumptions are discussed immediately with the project sponsor.

Chapter 10: Developing your own framework – A project plan

USING THIS report as a guide, you can now create a project plan for the design and implementation of a legal project management programme in your own firm or legal department. In this chapter, we will provide some practical advice on how to do this most effectively.

Threshold decisions

One of the first decisions to be made is whether the project management programme will be designed and developed in-house or by external consultants. This will involve an assessment of your timeline, your budget and your internal resources. You should consider your organisation's culture and its tolerance for outside expertise in areas traditionally in the exclusive purview of individual practitioners. Either approach can be effective. Dechert LLP and Seyfarth Shaw LLP engaged consultants to help design their programmes as described in Case studies 2 and 4. McCarthy Tétrault LLP chose to rely exclusively on internal resources, as described in Case study 1 (see Part Two of this report for case studies).

Setting objectives

As discussed in Chapter 4, successful projects start with clear and achievable objectives that will guide your planning. Your overall deliverable may be a project management programme in your firm; your objectives will be a list of specific outcomes that you hope to achieve with the project management initiative.

Your objectives should be realistic and consistent with your firm's strategic priorities. Potential objectives could include:

- Improving client service;
- Preparing the firm for the new pricing environment;
- Gaining a competitive advantage;
- Improving matter profitability; and
- Improving associate retention by providing a better work experience.

The project sponsor should consult as broadly as possible with members of the leadership team to ensure that the objectives are in line with the expectations of firm management. This will help gain the leadership support that will be critical to the success of the initiative.

It will be important to set objectives that are aligned with your firm culture as well. Improving matter profitability may be an objective that resonates with the majority of your partners. However, if this becomes your overriding focus, you must be prepared to have open discussions with lawyers about the impact of individual partner profit and overhead allocations on matter profitability. These issues can, in some firms, create controversy. In addition, the impact of associate leverage on matter profitability is something that your partners may understand well, but a discussion of this concept with associates can be far less comfortable. It may be easier to gain support from your associates by shifting the focus from profitability to the ways in which project management can improve their work experience.

Scope

In a law firm environment, you can expect individuals working on the project to have very different ideas about what ought to be done. Once the work begins, the temptation to veer out of scope by introducing new or 'better' approaches will be constant. Resist this. Some tips to keep the project on track are:

- Cede authority on all matters of scope to your project manager. He/she should have the power to shut down all discussions and reject all ideas with three simple words – 'out of scope'; and
- There will be many excellent ideas from the team that will nevertheless be out of scope. Create a place to keep these suggestions. This may be all that is necessary to close the issue and bring the discussions back on track.

What should and should not be included in the scope of the project will depend entirely on your objectives and timeline. There will be many potential law firm projects that are linked to project management that could be worthwhile inclusions. However, these can materially affect your timeline and resources, and should be considered carefully before they are included. The following are a few examples:

- Time recording incentives or penalties;
- Performance assessment tools;
- Risk or conflict management processes; and
- Diversity training.

The project plan

Once the objectives have been set, the project sponsor and the project manager should develop a project plan. It is a good idea to keep the project plan at a high level at first and to discuss it with your team before the detailed tasks and timelines are included.

A sample basic project plan could include:

- Developing a project management framework;
- Creating tools to support the framework;
- Creating training materials on the project management framework;
- Testing, piloting and improving the framework;
- Training all lawyers in the firm on the framework (rollout); and
- Tracking and reporting usage.

If this list looks daunting, consider dividing the plan into two separate projects. As described in Case study 3, Eversheds developed a complete project management framework for litigation matters before creating corresponding project management tools for transactional work.

You could consider dividing the development of the training and tools into one project and the training and tracking into another. You might consider using an outside consultant for the first project and an in-house project team for the second. However, the advantage to creating a single work team for the entire project is the ease with which you can refine the tools and training. For this reason, rather than creating two project teams, the work could be divided into phases (using the same project team for both), according to the specific skill sets that you consider most important to help you meet your overall objectives.

The timeline

Careful consideration should be given to a realistic timeframe for development and implementation of the initiative. Your project manager will be instrumental in setting and keeping the project on schedule.

The speed with which the market is moving away from traditional ways of buying legal services has set a demanding pace; you likely will not have the luxury of time. A few tips to deal with this are discussed further.

Tip one – Assess your organisation's existing tools

An audit of existing accounting, knowledge management, human resources and marketing systems may turn up some useful tools that can be brought under the project management umbrella. For example, many firms that do not have formal project management programmes do have pricing models to create fee estimates and costing models to calculate profits on a matter by matter basis. Some firms also have time recording systems that allow phase and task codes to be assigned on a practice type or matter basis. A thorough understanding of your firm's own systems before you start work could shorten your project timeline considerably.

Tip two – Look at what other firms are doing

If you are reading this report, you are already ahead of the game. The case studies in Part Two have been contributed by organisations that are leaders in this area and contain useful advice and ideas.

Tip three – Work on dual tracks

If you have divided the work into phases, you can improve your efficiency by creating two teams with timelines that run simultaneously. In this event, the two teams should have at least two members in common, and both teams should be overseen by the same steering committee.

Tip four – Accountability

The biggest threat to your timeline will be the competing pressure on the lawyers in your project team from clients to whom priority is (and should be) given. There is no best practice to deal with this conflict. However, there are several ways to create accountability for project deliverables that will help move them up a busy lawyer's to-do list:

- Decide on a convenient day and time for regular update meetings and schedule all of them in advance;
- Although the project sponsor is not normally part of the work team, this may well be a best practice for internal law firm projects. If the meetings are called and the agenda is set by the project sponsor, it will emphasise the importance of the meeting to the firm's overall strategic objectives; and
- Ensure that practice group leaders and support service managers are aware of the commitments and contributions made by the project team. Individual performance reviews should include an evaluation of contributions to the project.

Creative scheduling

When building the timeline, every effort should be made to design it around billable work commitments. The members of a project team in a law firm environment will require more flexibility than most standard timelines provide. Lawyers may prefer to take one or two days between cases or transactions to complete several deliverables at once. A weekend retreat for the entire team could also be a very effective and productive use of concentrated time.

Risks

It is important to identify the key risks you will face with the project, so that you can

Risks	Mitigation strategies
Lawyers will not see the value of project management to the firm or their individual practices	Include the business case in training and senior management communications; use real-life examples of successful pitches using project management
Lawyers will find the tools too difficult or time consuming to use	Make simplicity one of your overriding objectives in tool development
Lawyers will not be motivated to accept project management if it is not aligned with compensation or other rewards	Measure project management use and consider its use in compensation decisions
Client expectations of the impact of project management may be unrealistic	Run shadow project management pilots on client matters before any external commitments are made

Table 1: Key risks and mitigation strategies

consider how to address them before they occur, rather than waste valuable time and resources on damage control.

Table 1 highlights possible key risks and mitigations.

Assembling a project team

You will need to decide on the size and composition of your project team.

The first place to look for the necessary expertise is within your own firm. You will undoubtedly have partners who are known to have excellent file management skills. You may also have lawyers with engineering or technology backgrounds, who have used project management techniques earlier in their careers. In developing the project management module described in Case study 4, Seyfarth Shaw LLP drew on its existing project management resources – individuals who (until then) had experience mostly with internal firm projects.

It will be beneficial to have members of the team who have a thorough understanding of your organisation's knowledge management, information technology and accounting systems. If one of your objectives is to develop training, a member of your continuing legal education group should also be included.

Project management expertise may be more difficult to find in-house. As discussed in Chapter 2, there are certified project management professionals expert in both the theory and the practice of project management; however, they are unlikely to have any experience in the application of project management principles in a law firm. Do not be overly concerned by this. Resist the temptation to assume that the legal profession is unique and the principles espoused by project management professionals have no relevance to a legal practice. The lawyers on the project team will decide what is and what is not relevant to, or useful in, a legal practice. Be prepared for debates about this as individuals and individual practices differ.

Finding champions – The steering committee

It will be important to have a representative committee of partners from as many practice areas and offices as possible to steer the project team in the right direction. A steering committee should be created to act as an advisory board and provide feedback on the project at regular intervals. Ideally, this steering committee will be made up of many of your organisation's thought leaders and future champions of the initiative. Since they are often your busiest practitioners, they should understand that the time commitment required is relatively minimal. They will have no tasks assigned to them since their role is purely advisory. This will make it an attractive committee for most busy lawyers.

One of the key roles of a steering committee is that they be champions of the project and build support for the project in the firm. Gaining the support of the committee for the project will be a gradual and cumulative process and will require regular attendance at every meeting. Let them know how many meetings you expect to schedule and the amount of preparation needed. Be sure to set expectations for time commitments and ensure their role is clearly defined and agreed to.

The discussions at the committee meetings must be kept confidential until the project pilots are ready to launch. This may sound unnecessary, but it is without doubt a best practice. There will be many iterations of your project management programme and tools. Early leaks about any flaws could create a negative perception that would be difficult to overcome. The project team must be given the opportunity to bring all ideas to the steering committee and to act on any feedback. This is done most effectively in a confidential setting.

As important as it is to find early champions for the project, you should also have a few cynics on the steering committee. These members may be more representative of the common view than those who are prepared to keep an open mind. If you can turn cynics into supporters, it will pay enormous dividends when you are ready to launch the project. If you are not able to win them over, you will have time during the confidentiality period to develop a mitigation strategy before the project is launched.

Finally, it is a good idea to have a very senior member of management recruit the steering committee and obtain commitments from each member. This will impress upon them the importance of the role and should make potential members think twice before making commitments that they are not able to meet. This will increase the accountability needed to keep the project on track and on time.

Administrative support

The extent to which you rely on the firm's non-lawyer resources will depend on a number of factors, both operational and cultural.

Most firms have service organisations that deal with operational aspects of the business and provide different kinds of support to the legal professionals. Many of the more senior members of the service organisation will have commercial backgrounds that make them well suited to the project team and, eventually, to participate in the pricing and monitoring stages of specific legal mandates.

Consideration should be given to forming a support team of senior members of your finance and information technology departments, who are available to assist legal professionals as they familiarise themselves with the new tools. For a comprehensive discussion of the growing importance of the law firm back office and the key role played by administrative resource groups, please refer to Case study 2.

The larger law firms in the UK have understood the benefits of integrating non-legal support staff with practising lawyers. In fact, although many UK firms may not have formal project management programmes, they do have highly-skilled business managers who work with lawyers and who are involved in the pricing and monitoring of large mandates.

Collaboration of this sort between legal and non-legal professionals is common in some firms and rarely seen in others. Firms that do not have a history of working in an integrated way with their non-legal support staff may choose to keep their support team standing by. There is a high probability that this support team's help will be sought by busy lawyers who may be struggling with unfamiliar concepts or software. Over time, these individuals could assume more of a leading role and may become the project managers on future mandates.

The communication plan

Given the non-hierarchical structure of law partnerships, even the most important management initiatives sometimes have trouble gaining traction. This is particularly true of new programmes or tools that involve training sessions. Careful attention should be paid to the way the initiative is portrayed, both internally and externally. As word spreads, you could see a groundswell of support or a wall of resistance. A proper communication plan can make the difference.

The focus of your communication plan will change over the life of the project. At the outset, you will need to focus on the business case and your specific objectives for introducing a formal project management initiative. It will help to create speaking points for all those involved, so that the message is clear and consistent. Support from senior management should be commutated regularly through your organisation's usual channels, including partners meetings and firm-wide e-mails.

An internal website dedicated to project management can facilitate communication of all aspects of your programme, including updates on the development and refinements of tools, templates and training materials. Regular e-mails can be sent reminding lawyers that tools and templates are available for use on client matters. These communications should stress that legal project management can be useful in planning and pricing existing work, but also in pitches for new work. Once the programme has been running for a sufficient length of time, the focus of communication will shift to the sharing of success stories. Client feedback, successful pitches and well-managed transactions or cases are all good examples that can be shared firm wide.

As you will note from the case studies in Part Two, many of the leading firms that use project management have chosen names for their initiatives in order to create a recognisable brand in the market. Seyfarth Shaw uses 'Seyfarth*Lean*' to highlight its adherence to 'Six Sigma Lean' principles. Eversheds uses 'RAPID' for its litigation management model and McCarthy Tétrault has 'Dialogue Project Management™'. While project management is relatively new in the legal profession, firms that are able to achieve this sort of brand recognition will have a significant competitive advantage.

Opportunities for market differentiation do not present themselves every day. Although designing and implementing a legal project management programme in your firm or legal department may seem like an overwhelming challenge, the real challenge is coming from your clients. In the current environment, lawyers must be able to work with reliable fee estimates or, in many cases, an overall fixed price. They must have the skills and tools to manage these engagements whilst at the same time ensure the firm's profitability.

Accepting this new business reality is the first step. Responding to it by investing time and resources in project management is the next. The benefits will follow.

PART TWO

Case Studies

Case study 1: McCarthy Tétrault LLP – Legal project management – A strategic priority for the firm

A strategic initiative

After completing a firm-wide process to articulate our firm's brand, we came to a humbling conclusion. Although most of us would prefer to be known for our legal excellence, it became apparent that the way we work – not what we do – is what distinguishes us in an increasingly competitive market. Clients are now making hiring decisions by assessing the overall experience with their law firms, not simply the narrow legal outcome.

Clients place a high value on well-managed matters for a variety of reasons. Cost predictability has become particularly important in the current economy where budgets are constrained and clients want more control over the cost and other outcomes of their legal matters. We saw an opportunity to provide a better experience and enhanced value to our clients by introducing project management to our lawyers.

Keeping it simple

We began with a small work team and a few ideas. Simplicity was our overriding goal. We did not set out to build the perfect machine but rather, one that our lawyers would actually use. We made a few judgment calls that set the direction for the initiative.

First, we believed that our lawyers would reject an imported project management system and decided to develop the programme entirely in-house, using our own internal resources. We were fortunate to have a certified project management professional with engineering and information technology development expertise in our firm. All of our supporting software was developed in-house. Although there are more sophisticated products available, we chose to develop our tools using Microsoft Excel since it was familiar to our lawyers and easy to use. To facilitate the use of Excel in a project management model, it was necessary to layer custom code in the background to allow lawyers and their assistants, with only basic knowledge of Excel, to use the tools.

Second, we stripped virtually all of the project management jargon out of our model. Where we did not see a material benefit in following strict project management theory, we ignored it. Where we saw value in adopting specific project management terminology, we explained why.

For example, we adopted the concept of a project 'sponsor' to highlight the difference between the client and the specific individual at the client (for example, the general counsel), who will define the project objectives, timeline, scope and cost, and can be accountable for the outcome. The sponsor will assess the success of the mandate from his/her personal perspective and will make the next hiring decision accordingly. Looking at a matter from the perspective of a project sponsor is a fundamentally important discipline in effective project management and could make the difference between winning and losing the next engagement from your client.

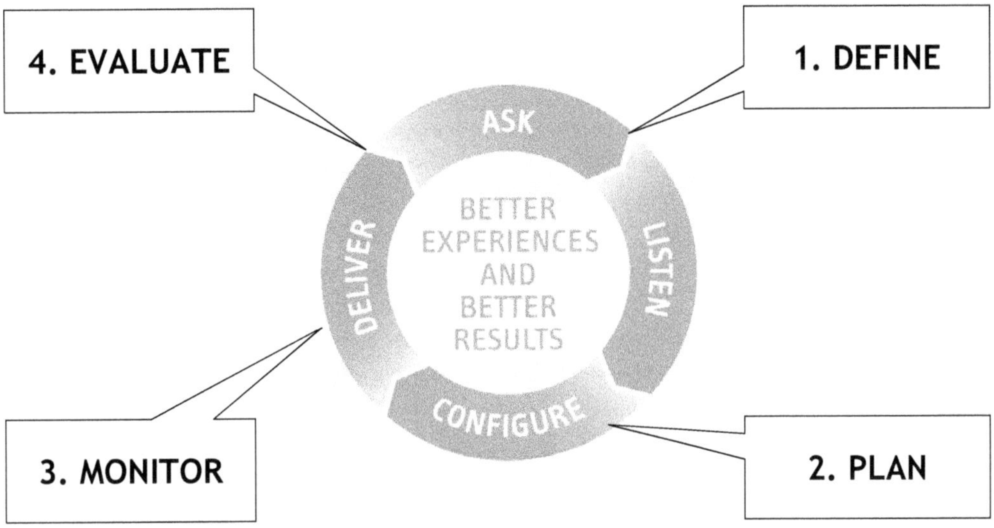

Figure 1: The Dialogue Project Management™ model

Third, we took our time and conducted many pilots in various offices, using the feedback we received to refine our programme. After a significant period of development and testing, we were ready to launch a comprehensive set of proprietary tools and matter management techniques we called 'Dialogue Project Management™'.

Dialogue Project Management™

Under the Dialogue Project Management™ model, our lawyers will continue to supervise and perform legal work as they have always done, but they now have the additional responsibility of acting as project manager. They are responsible for managing the mandate in accordance with the model outlined in Figure 1.

The inner circle is a graphic that was already familiar to our lawyers and depicts the service delivery model that we established as part of a firm-wide initiative to articulate our brand. It is a graphic representation of the way we work with clients and with each other.

We have superimposed a legal project management model onto our own service delivery model. The outer squares depict the four stages of a project and represent the specific project management responsibilities. Those responsibilities can, and in many cases should, be delegated, but the lead lawyer will always be accountable for the results.

The role of the project manager

The project manager is obviously a key player in our model. We considered who should play this role and whether the role was better performed by a lawyer or a trained business or project manager. After considering many factors, including our existing internal resources and firm culture, we decided that the lead lawyer on a matter should also be the project manager. However, once the project had been properly defined in a scope document, all of the administrative responsibilities of the project manager could then be delegated to an appropriate resource. Some of these responsibilities could be assumed by another lawyer on the team or a member of our support staff – or both. Accountability for all four stages of the matter would nevertheless remain with the lead lawyer.

Tools

Our Dialogue Project Management™ toolbox was designed using the Project Management Institute (PMI) best practices and some of our own. It has three principal components with three different primary functions, and they are discussed further.

Planning tools

We used simple Excel-based tools for a series of customised work plan templates. Each transaction or case-specific template has been built by the lawyers who use them. This involved a significant investment of professional resources, but resulted in templates which practitioners find useful and in which they are prepared to place a high level of trust.

Template development is an ongoing process at our firm that occurs at the practice and industry group level. We have a library of work-plan templates available for each of the major types of work that we do. They contain a checklist of tasks and deliverables required on a particular matter and identify the different levels of resources (for example, partner, mid-level associate, paralegal, etc.) available in the firm to perform the tasks. The exercise for the lawyer planning the matter is to identify the appropriate resource and to estimate the number of hours required to perform each task.

The work plan templates are linked to our various knowledge management resources. We have built some helpful estimating functions and tools into all work plan templates that are available if needed. Each template also includes a list of general assumptions that should be considered when creating a work plan.

Staffing tool

Once the work plan has been completed, the information may be moved automatically to our staffing tool. This is a firm-wide database of all our professionals categorised under practice area, home office and hourly rates. Lawyers can choose the individuals from a drop-down menu to staff the matter. The tool will calculate a fee estimate that can be used as a budget for the matter.

We chose to separate the planning and staffing tools to encourage lawyers to consider what level of professional was appropriate for a task before choosing the individuals to do the work. By imposing this discipline, we increase the odds that the right work will be done at the right level, which is often more cost effective for the client and is always more professionally satisfying for the lawyers working on the matter.

Monitoring tools

Our monitoring tools are being developed in two phases. We currently use a manual system while our longer-term automated system is being developed.

For clients that do not use electronic billing, we use the phase and task code capabilities of our existing billing systems and map them to the phases and tasks of work plans. Projects are monitored by phase, unless otherwise requested by our clients. Since billing information is entered in our system at the time of docketing, it is available to billing lawyers through our existing matter financial portal. It is fairly simple for an administrative assistant to re-enter this billing information into an Excel-based monitoring worksheet (an example is provided in the sample monitoring worksheet provided in Part One, Chapter 7 of this report).

We are currently building a longer-term system to allow our client's electronic billing phase and task codes to be mapped to our work plan phase and task codes. We are also developing an additional capability that allows key information from the work plan to also be placed in our billing systems. This additional data will allow us to present a real-time report of budget against actual costs automatically through our financial portal.

Training

We used our own senior lawyers and a certified project management professional to conduct the training sessions. We did this to build credibility, increase attendance and demonstrate the usefulness of the tools to lawyers.

We began our training with a general session on project management fundamentals that focused on the Dialogue Project Management™ model. We discussed changing market pressures and positioned project management as our firm's proactive response. We also demonstrated the tools, using a generic case study. Once we had trained all of our partners, we held similar sessions for our associates and paralegals. All sessions were conducted live in each of our offices. The training was not mandatory in the strictest sense, but it was required before access to the tools could be granted.

The second phase of the training was done at the practice and industry-group level using a work plan template and case study that was developed specifically for the particular area of practice. These were run (and continue to run) as workshops and are intended to give lawyers hands-on experience with the tools.

Consulting with clients

Since we began the initiative as a way to deliver better value to our clients, we took the direct approach and asked them if what we were developing was valuable to them. We conducted a series of short presentations to certain key clients in all of our offices. We presented our Dialogue Project Management™ framework and provided a short demonstration of our proprietary tools. We were very interested in receiving comments from our clients on the value of our approach and gained much positive feedback on our initiative.

While some law firms were exploring the idea of legal project management, our clients told us that very few firms had the systems or tools to manage matters in the way our firm was proposing. This was useful information for us, as it confirmed our initial view that we could differentiate the firm by offering a new way of working that was more aligned with our clients' business interests.

External communications – Branding

The feedback we received at our client presentations, including the comments relating to the innovative nature of the programme led to an internal exercise to create an appropriate 'brand' for our model. This required us to take a hard look at the programme in order to articulate its essential characteristics. We were looking for a name that would be descriptive and meaningful to our own lawyers, to our clients and to the broader legal services market. We chose 'Dialogue' because of the prominence given to regular and effective communication at every stage of our model. The importance of a constant dialogue with clients throughout a matter was a central theme in our training and implementation. It was also something that our clients mentioned in our early presentations as the key to making project management work.

The importance of internal communication

Although external communications are clearly important, internal communications are also critical with any new initiative. In the early days before the idea had gained much ground, we described the business case and objectives of project management at partners' meetings in all of our offices. We provided updates as the programme developed. We chose our pilot groups carefully – recruiting lawyers who we believed would give us honest feedback and who would also be vocal in their support of the programme if they believed it to be useful to their practices. Eventually, project management became one of our firm's two highest strategic priorities and was on the agenda for virtually all of our partners' meetings. Our CEO, Marc-Andre Blanchard, is a vocal supporter of Dialogue Project Management™ and speaks about it internally and externally at every opportunity.

Now that the launch of project management is well underway, the internal communication plan has shifted to sharing improvements to the tools and success stories. We also have a well developed intranet site where work plan templates for our major transactions are available to all of our lawyers. It contains links to other useful checklists and tools, resource materials, web-based training and media coverage.

Dialogue Project Management™ in practice

We thought it would be appropriate to conclude this case study with examples of Dialogue Project Management™ in practice.

We were asked to provide a quote on the various aspects of a litigation matter. We prepared a work plan breaking it down by phases and tasks, and provided a cost estimate by phase. Our client was initially sceptical and expressed some surprise at the size of the original estimate. This led to a series of detailed discussions with the project sponsor that allowed him to understand all of the tasks and time involved, and to make decisions as to what to prioritise. It was important to the project sponsor for us to back up some of the estimates with empirical data from prior experience. Both our client and the project sponsor were very satisfied with the management of the matter and provided unsolicited positive feedback with respect to the benefits they perceived, including:

- Better cost predictability;
- Control; and
- Communication.

It was the first experience with legal project management for both the lead partner on that matter and our client, and they both viewed it as successful.

Another client, a major international corporation, had begun to move much of its more routine corporate work to lower-cost firms. Our firm was invited to pitch for the legal work to integrate a newly-acquired business into our client's operations. The partner in charge decided to submit a bid with a very detailed work plan complete with timelines and assumptions, together with a fee estimate based upon the use of our tools. We were told that we were the only firm to quote using legal project management and were awarded the mandate not because we were the lowest quote, but because our client felt that our bid provided the most certainty and control over the process. In other words, cost predictability, together with the significant engagement of the project sponsor, were the key drivers. The cost was higher than originally quoted, but the potential for the cost overrun was identified and communicated to the project sponsor early, together with an explanation of which facts in the underlying assumptions had changed. Our client paid the bill in full and was satisfied with the process.

We believe that this positive experience will lead to increased work from this client.

Case study 2: Dechert LLP – Developing best practice in legal project management

By Ben Barnett, partner and Colleen Nilhill, director of project management, Dechert LLP

DECHERT LLP (Dechert) launched its formal project management initiative in the Autumn of 2009 in response to client demands for greater value and efficiency in delivering legal services. Based on a belief that all our clients would benefit from enhanced project management expertise and support, we engaged one of the leading legal consultants in the field to train all of our partners in project management. This training is now being offered to all of our legal professionals, including associates, support staff and paralegals.

Consistent with our client-focused philosophy, we routinely review our matters with our clients with respect to project performance for feedback. This 'After Action Review' enables us to continually improve our project management processes by adding further efficiencies. Valuable lessons can be learned from project successes as well as from projects that, despite best efforts, do not go as planned. This section of the case study is a discussion of best practices developed from some of these lessons.

Dechert's commitment to its project management initiative goes well beyond training. Dechert has established a dedicated team of administrative personnel, led by its director of project management to support its project management initiative. Further in this case study, a description of the infrastructure that Dechert has built around its project management programme is offered. This infrastructure has enabled the firm to provide its lawyers with the tools and resources to actively and efficiently manage matters.

The six lessons learned

Any discussion of best practices for project management is incomplete without acknowledging the other side of the coin – that despite our experience and best efforts on behalf of our clients, projects do not always go as planned. Deadlines get missed, budgets get stretched and the end product does not satisfy either our clients or ourselves. The challenge is to view and treat such mistakes as a real opportunity to learn, so that in the future, you can improve your performance and that of your team for the benefit of your clients.

Lesson one – You can't do what you don't define

In the after glow and rush of a new client matter, scant attention is normally paid to defining specifically what the client has retained you to do. This oversight can haunt and even derail the entire project. Most of the problems in project management have their genesis in the failure to define. This is particularly true in the current alternative fee environment. The temptation, particularly with new clients, is to simply add more and more work for a flat fee to demonstrate flexibility and alignment. While that may be a perfectly-sound business development model, it comes at a potential cost to your firm. So-called mission creep can wreck both your schedules and your realisation, potentially angering your clients and your colleagues. There is also a risk that you will not deliver specifically what the client wants – which is not a recipe for future retention.

The way to overcome this is to sit down in person with the appropriate decision makers immediately after retention and set out in writing the following:

- The overall objective of the project;
- The specific steps that you and your team will take to reach that objective; and
- The budget.

While this process is both predictive and iterative, you must hammer out these three building blocks.

Lesson two – Building a team to be its best

Another initial critical step is to determine who is going to be on your team for the project. Your success will largely be driven by your team. Making sound staffing decisions requires consideration of innumerable factors, including:

- The schedule and budget;
- Technical knowledge or knowledge of the client;
- Past performance; and
- Commitment.

The temptation, particularly for counsel without substantial project management experience, is to rely on your go-to team or a large group of lawyers because there is security (largely false) in numbers.

Do your best to resist this temptation because it can lead to under performance by the team and mid-project personnel issues. About a year ago, I selected a lawyer to head up a sub-team. He had over five years of experience handling a specific task. The selection was easy (he knew the client and knew what we were doing) but it was not the right selection. Had I been better attuned to the signals, I would have realised that he viewed the work as limiting his career and he was burned out after five years of managing a difficult, but not professionally-rewarding task. Half-way through the project, he had to be replaced. Asking team members to do the same task day after day is not necessarily good for a project's success or individuals' careers.

You should also be ruthless in terms of what resources you really need on your team. Consider the US Army's experience on Omaha Beach during the D-Day invasion. If you read most historic accounts (official and unofficial), they pinpoint success on that day as being the result of very small units of soldiers (many from different units), who banded together and worked out a way to get off the beach under nearly impossible odds. Sometimes you need an army, but sometimes you only need two or three dedicated, focused people.

You owe it to your client, your team and yourself to devote the necessary time and attention to the staffing of your team. Keep the team as small as possible and remember that (most) lawyers welcome and are energised by personal and professional challenges. Equally, don't lose sight of unit cohesion and reward those who work well with the client and others on the team. Finally, don't be complacent – if it is not working, fix it immediately.

Lesson three – The nuts and bolts

While executing the work seems an obvious point to raise, you might be surprised by how many teams struggle in the area of getting the work done. While some teams are great at planning and conducting team meetings and carrying out exhaustive (and exhausting) discussions, they fall down on actual execution. Execution is what separates good and great project management teams.

Clients pay for our project management teams to perform. One wise and experienced in-house paralegal told me that she largely judges outside firms' performance on two criteria:

- How they treat each other and other firms; and
- How many emergencies arose during an assignment.

In-fighting or inter-firm strife are a distraction from reaching the project's objectives and can cost clients time and resources. Similarly, multiple or continuous emergencies are not a sign of commitment rather, they are a sign of poor management or leadership.

Many work performance issues can be addressed by having in place a concrete project plan and appropriate staffing. Beyond that, these issues start and stop at the top with the project manager. Lead by example. Don't engage in, or tolerate intra or inter-firm political fights. If someone is struggling to meet deadlines, identify what help they need to put them back on track. Reward candour and credibility and don't engage in, or permit inter-personal conflicts to distract you or your team from the client-defined objectives.

Lesson four – Where are we?

Any project management process taken to an extreme can be counterproductive. On the other hand, most sophisticated clients will expect you to be able to report your progress on a regular and real-time basis. Given this level of expectation, you should build into your initial project plan agreed-upon interim deadlines. Such benchmarks will provide several benefits:

- Keeping your team focused on the overall project objective;
- Tracking your progress; and
- Improving your contingency planning if (or when) you encounter challenges not identified in your original project plan.

In creating your reporting structure, ask to see internal company reports as there can be real currency in using the same software or format.

Working backwards from your delivery date, agree to a set of interim deadlines on which you will report your progress to the client. Getting such agreement in advance (subject to reasonable flexibility) is critical. In one recent project that we handled for a new client, the client came back after we had scoped the project and began asking for more and more interim reports because of the increasing visibility of the project within the company. For obvious reasons, we did the additional interim reports, but they distracted us from the overall project and the agreed deliverables, required us to spend more hours than originally budgeted and reduced our overall realisation of the project. You need to avoid (as best as you can) death by a thousand reports.

Lesson five – Planning for problems

Despite all your planning and active management, the chances are something will go wrong during the life of your project. The critical question is how much impact will those problems have on your project or client relationship. While it is natural to try to immediately delve into whom or what caused the problem, fight that urge because how you respond to the problem is actually far more important to both the project and the client relationship.

While you can't plan to completely avoid problems, you can create a plan for rapid response and resolution by your team. Again, encourage and demand candour from team members to speak up before issues become problems. Once a problem arises, identify as best as you can the cause (no witch hunts or congressional hearings) and several alternative solutions. You should then assess whether the issue is one that the client needs to know about and whether they need to approve the proposed solution. If the answer to either question is yes, then inform the client immediately and provide a specific recommendation. Once you are satisfied that the agreed-upon solution is working, talk with your team about how to avoid the same or similar problems in the future.

Lesson six – Delivering success

Many legal professionals think that the hard work on project management is done when they deliver the final work product to the client. The most critical phase of long-term successful project management happens after delivery of the final product – a step that most often gets short shrift. If you or your team has learned nothing from the experience, nothing that could benefit this or another client, then you have not delivered success. Every project is an opportunity to do a better job for your clients and build the project management skills of everyone on your team. Your collective success depends on learning from both your achievements and mistakes.

After you complete the project, there needs to be at least two conversations with respect to the project:

- One external discussion with the client; and
- One internal discussion with your team.

With respect to the external discussion, you need to request a meeting with the client where you can spend time discussing the project in detail – what went right, what went wrong and what you might consider doing differently in the future. If the client asks for feedback with respect to the client team, respect the request and ask the same of them. Consider bringing key team members to such a meeting as both a reward and to expand their exposure and experience with clients. Then, have a meeting (ideally, over a meal) with your team and invite everyone to provide feedback with respect to both the project and the team, with the stated goal of improving both individual and team performance in the future.

The value of support departments

What happens after legal project management training has finished and the commencement of the initiative begins? This question puzzles most firms.

Good legal project management starts with partners fully understanding their clients' needs. They have to marry those business needs with first-rate legal counsel, in part, by creating a work plan and a budget and managing these. This sounds obvious since most lawyers have been practising this for years.

Clients today, however, demand more frequent and detailed communication as their matters proceed. Moreover, they are asking for information about the progression of their matters in ways in which most lawyers are not typically trained and, in some cases, do not entirely understand. It is in this area of information assembly and presentation where good administrative support intersects with legal project management and why typically back-office departments are of growing importance in law firms.

The law firm support departments that have been particularly helpful in ensuring a successful legal project management launch are discussed further.

Finance

In the wake of the recession, most CEOs have grown even stricter about budget control. Historically, tight cost control measures were not rigorously applied to legal departments. In-house legal budgets seemed to expand to fit whatever law firms charged. Now, many general counsel are under the same pressures as their corporate counterparts and are asking their outside counsel to stop speaking legalese and start slinging corporate jargon. Part of this shift includes providing detailed budgets broken down to include phases, tasks, major deliverables, key time frames and necessary resources. In order to provide a budget that is both appealing to the client and profitable for a firm, it is critical that finance personnel be involved at the outset.

Lawyers obviously have to use their judgment in determining the way that a matter should be structured and how it should be staffed. Finance can help by turning tasks and hours into an overall budget and use modelling measures to create various types of billing arrangements that work with the clients' overall financial constraints – standard rate, fixed fees, capped fee, volume discount, just to name a few.

Once a fee structure is chosen and a budget is established, it essential to manage to that budget. Lawyers cannot do this in a vacuum. They need to receive regular reporting so they can analyse deltas between the budget and the actual run rates. For example, if an associate is budgeted to work on a particular client task for a certain amount of time, it is critical that the supervising lawyer receives feedback about whether the associate is working within the established guidelines. Reconciling the budget with the bill at the month's end hinders the ability to make real-time changes and limits the ability to give advance warning of changes to the client. The headache lawyers have sifting through time entries and Excel reports can be alleviated by a trained financial analyst, who can focus partners on areas of concern.

Knowledge management

Creating the first budget or work plan is a giant hurdle. Lawyers crave precedent and their law school training encourages them to start with something that has been tried and tested. Budgets and work plans, however, are not something that a consultant can design and craft as a template, nor are they something that should be drafted by administrative personnel. They should be the by-product of a lawyer's detailed communication with their client and a reflection of their legal judgment and experience.

However, it is always helpful to have someone with a finance background or a full-time devoted project management professional pair with a lawyer to take their words and create something more formal, like a Gantt chart or a process map (see Appendix 1 for an example of a Gantt chart). Unfortunately, if lawyers can't easily find this information, some of them hesitate to start from scratch and fail to engage in the exercise at all.

Knowledge management departments best serve legal project management initiatives when they are focused on setting up a process of recalling previously-designed budgets or work plans. Instead of reinventing the wheel, a lawyer can visit a virtual library and look through prior example budgets that his/her peers have designed. In order to populate a warehouse with this kind of information, there must be clearly-communicated protocols established to encourage a sharing environment. Those protocols should not just be directives that are e-mailed to the lawyers, but suggestions coupled with champions who benefited from this approach.

Practice group administration

Some firms have directors who oversee the business functions of each of their practice groups. These individuals best understand their groups' personality. They are embedded in the practice area and, in some cases, develop business strategy. Since legal project management isn't a one-size-fits-all type of approach, it is particularly important to have someone who can offer counsel on how to best tailor the message to comply with specific industry needs. For example, when monitoring a budget, litigators seem to be interested in having a granular understanding of how their timekeepers are progressing on each task. Their corporate colleagues, who have shorter matter cycle lengths, prefer to see less detailed reports. The differences in the type of information they need obviously affect the type of reporting that the lawyers should be provided and what other administrative support might follow. A recommended approach when considering a legal project management roll out in a multidisciplinary firm is to fully understand the practice group's client base and to engage the practice group director to align reporting, marketing and training strategies.

Professional development

Training cannot stop as soon as the consultants walk out of the door. An ongoing effort to train lateral and incoming junior associates must be part of an overall strategy in the roll out of a legal project management initiative. Legal project management is not a binder of material that lawyers take from a training session with a consultant and then shelve. It should be a way of carrying out client matters that is weaved into the firm's overall fabric. This starts by regularly scheduling training programmes. Just as important is taking legal project management behaviours and including them as part of the critical skills necessary to progress through a firm. Similarly, supervising lawyers should be rewarded for encouraging their team to promptly respond to client requests, properly prioritising assignments and demonstrating efficiencies.

Marketing

The business development responsibilities of a marketing department are fairly obvious in response to a client-friendly initiative like legal project management. Perhaps a less apparent role is the internal marketing to the firm's own lawyers. One way to accomplish this in-house public relation effort is to regularly publish success stories and create a dedicated legal project management intranet site. The site works best when there are current articles, client-focused materials for requests for proposals and 'wins' that the firm has experienced. It is not imperative to wait until a giant client of the firm sings praises about how efficient its team of lawyers have been. It is equally or more important to celebrate even small successes such as an associate receiving positive feedback from a smaller client who is pleased with the efficiencies they are seeing as a result of a closely-monitored work plan and budget.

Project management – A department in itself?

Coordinating the aforementioned departments so that they act in concert can prove to be quite a challenge, not unlike the metaphoric herding of cats. Law firms truly committed to investing in legal project management initiatives as opposed to merely reacting to the PR buzz on a superficial level, however, have expanded their infrastructure to include a department solely dedicated to legal project management. In order to be effective and successful, legal project management departments need to be staffed and managed by people who understand law firm culture. Specifically, legal project management department heads must be able to identify both the areas in which long-standing business principles, commonplace in corporations, can benefit a law firm and where such principles simply have no place within a law firm setting.

While some firms recognise the need for a coordinated legal project management department after training ceases, the preferable approach is to start with a legal project management director. Best practices suggest that this legal project management director should take responsibility for choosing the training approach. Most firms toil with whether to have training programmes run by outside consultants or a crew of firm lawyers and staff who display a project management aptitude. A legal project management director would be able to recognise that it is not an either-or approach. Consultants provide a great benefit and tend to establish credibility by bringing industry experience and the client voice to bear. Lawyers and support staff, however, are equally necessary and should be involved in the legal project management initiatives roll out.

Firms which established legal project management departments are novel right now, but that is not likely to remain the case. As the economy heals, we are likely to see corporate counsel still demanding demonstrable project management capabilities of their outside legal counsel. That client-driven requirement should not be thought of as a burden that a law firm must bear, but as an opportunity to build better relationships with clients by speaking their language.

Ben Barnett is partner and Colleen Nilhill is director of project management at Dechert LLP. They can be contacted at: ben.barnett@dechert.com and colleen.nilhill@dechert.com, respectively

Case study 3: Eversheds LLP – Achieving certainty in cost, scope and time

By Kevin Doolan, partner and Paul Smith, partner, Eversheds LLP

Project management origins in litigation

Eversheds LLP (Eversheds) began its journey into project management as a result of its membership of the 'DuPont Partner Law Firm Network'. Eversheds was the first international law firm to join the network some 12 years ago and the various elements of the DuPont Legal Model have been incorporated into the practice of the firm.

At the outset, the firm incorporated the 'Early Case Assessment' model into its approach to litigation, providing a strategy and the 'Best Practical Outcomes' (BPO) for a client within the first 30 days of being instructed. The methodology was adapted by Eversheds to include the entire life cycle of a litigation matter with a regular review of the strategy which the firm branded as 'RAPID' – Review, Analyse, Plan, Implement and Deliver.

Before RAPID, our research with clients had found that they often felt that litigation was full of uncertainties – it was impossible to create a clear budget and it tended to go out of clients' control. At the start of a dispute, little or no attention had been given to what might be the possible length or cost of the case or what different paths it might follow. RAPID resolved this by the following:

- A detailed month-by-month analysis of the likely course of the dispute on the assumption that it went all the way to trial;
- A month-by-month budget of costs and disbursements; and
- A professional opinion, based on the evidence so far, of what was the BPO for the dispute.

This enabled the client to make a reasoned judgement, taking into account all of the relevant factors and to communicate with the relevant business unit in a way that they could understand. Once that business unit saw the full cost of going all the way to trial, it helped them make a rational business decision. For example, a decision might be that a settlement at between cost X and cost Y in month seven (just before a very large expenditure on discovery took place) would be the best solution.

Those who were not familiar with 'Early Case Assessment' might say that litigation was impossible to predict or to sensibly budget. However, that misses the point – this is not an attempt to predict, but to gather all the information that is available so that the current best path can be chosen. Further, the RAPID document is living – amendments can be made as new facts or circumstances arise, new timelines and budgets can be produced and this will lead to another discussion on what is the BPO. Actions can then follow that route.

At the time, it gave the client a very clear choice – use a firm that will use 'Early Case Assessment'/RAPID as a structural approach, which enables you to continuously monitor options and spend, or use a firm which

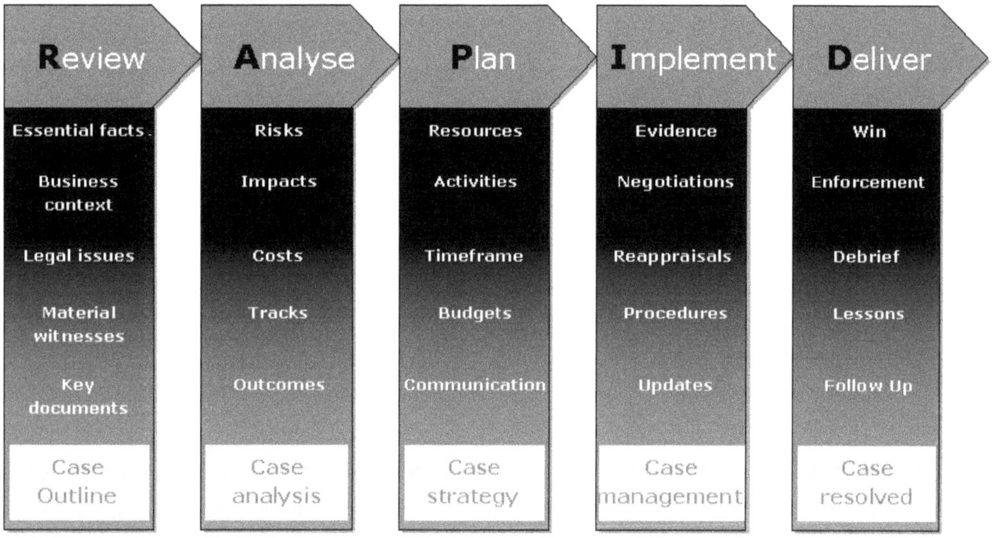

Figure 1: Eversheds RAPID process

says 'litigation is too uncertain to predict'. Eversheds also tracked the results of RAPID. One exercise, which was taking 100 recently-finished litigation cases to see what results had actually been achieved, found that in 91 of the cases, the end result was the agreed BPO.

Training

A lot of work went into creating the methodology behind RAPID. It represented a considerable change for the firm, because in systematising the approach to litigation, it meant that very clear procedures had to be followed and templates used. Every litigation team in the firm was involved in feeding into the system, so that it gathered all of the technical expertise of the firm. A major training exercise took place over a two-year period to make sure that every lawyer was equipped with this new approach – creating a project plan and then delivering against it.

What was most interesting was that even some of the very best litigation lawyers were weak when it came to estimating costs. This was because the data from previous cases had not been captured, so it was extremely difficult to give clear guidance on the likely month-by-month costs of similar matters. Without robust data, broken down into every category of case, any estimates were unlikely to be accurate, so a key stage was to create a detailed and regularly-updated database which lawyers could consult, in order to create a realistic case plan and budget. Training took place across all grades and led to the creation of online tools, so that entry of key factors about a case started to create a detailed case timeline and budget.

The end result

The most valuable end result of using project management tools on litigation has been to create an intelligent conversation between the lawyer and the client (and typically also the client's relevant business unit). This conversation would be along the lines of, 'We dealt with X hundred similar cases over the last XX years. On average, the matters lasted for eight months and cost £XX,000. The best case finished after two months and cost £XX,000 and the longest went to trial and lasted 30 months in total at a cost of

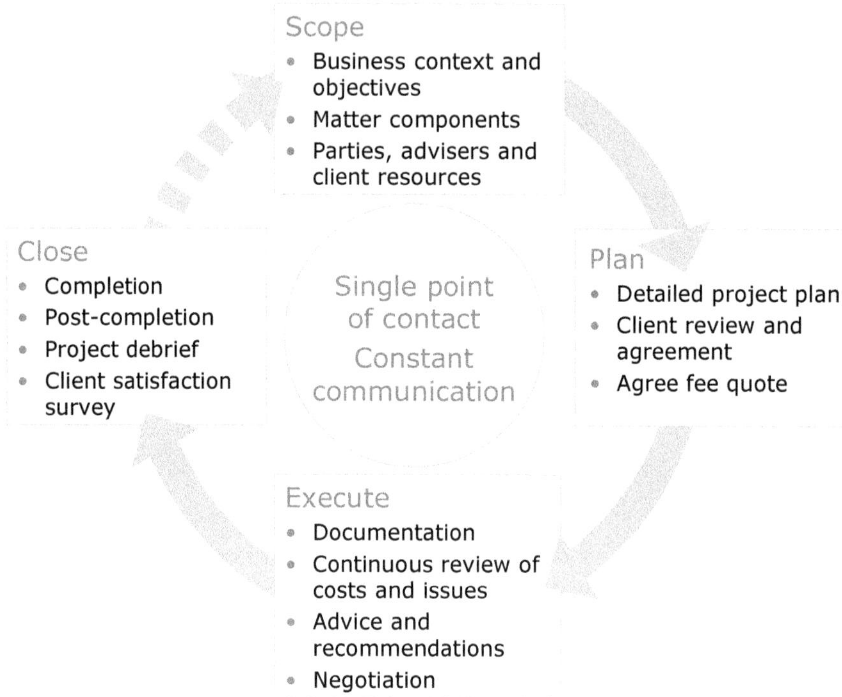

Figure 2: The four-stage project management process

£Xm. Based upon the information that we have gathered so far, we think that a realistic budget for this case is £XX,000 and that the BPO will be a settlement in the sum of £Xm in month ten.'

Using project management in non-contentious work

Client reaction to the project management of litigation cases using RAPID was very positive. Clearly, if this could be provided in litigation, then it should also be possible in transactional work. The next stage of the journey for Eversheds was to create corresponding project management tools for non-contentious work. The starting point was merger and acquisitions (M&A) transactions which led to the development of what was called 'DealTrack'. This was based upon a four-stage process – Scoping; Planning; Executing; and Closing – and can be illustrated in Figure 2.

The model was based upon being able to answer the following questions:

- Have we agreed with our client what they want and what we are going to do (by explaining our approach, properly scoping the work and understanding the key issues)?
- Have we told the client how much it is going to cost (by providing them with a written budget which we will adhere to, provided the work involved does not stray beyond the agreed scope and assumptions)?
- Have we ensured that all of the staff involved know what the job is about and what they have to do (by holding briefing meetings)?
- Have we kept the client informed of key issues and costs on a regular and agreed basis? and
- At the end of the job, have we arranged for a formal independent satisfaction

survey? Are there lessons for us that will help us to improve on delivery of the next piece of work?

The project management resources

There were three pillars for success. First, there needed to be a clear and agreed methodology for every separate work type with written processes and procedures that would be followed by the whole team. Secondly, the lawyers needed to be trained in delivering (project managing what was often a large team across a complex project). Thirdly, there needed to be databases capturing details of previous transactions – in fact, this led again to the development of online tools to ensure the creation of reliable project plans and budgets.

Benefits for the client

Resolving the issue of scope and cost

There was a need for detailed scoping conversations at the start of the matter so that the project plan and budget could be created. This flushed out any issue over scope and cost. In fact, it was not a problem if the client said that they had budgeted much less than what was being planned by Eversheds. The great amount of detail in the initial project plan and budget could mean that the client re-assessed the amount of work that was going to be needed and (often in conjunction with the client's business unit) agreed to the necessary work and the cost. Alternatively, the scope of work would be reduced so that the budget dropped. It may be that the client was happy for some areas to be excluded or would agree to carry out that work in-house. In either case, it meant that there was a clearly agreed scope and budget on day one. (Compare that with finding out that there was a major difference in understanding that only emerges at completion of a matter when the final bill is presented.)

The client is in control

Eversheds' responsibility was to deliver the agreed project scope for the agreed project budget. The total cost could only increase on two conditions. First, there had to be a change in the scope of work meaning extra work was required. Secondly, Eversheds had to give a quote for the extra work before it was carried out, and the client had to agree that they wanted the extra work. This gave the client the option not to have any extra scope and cost – again because they might take a commercial risk on an issue or might decide to carry out any extra work in house

Speaking the client's language

Perhaps, above all, legal project management meant that there could be no surprises either in scope or cost. Clients have said, time and again, that this was the greatest benefit of a project management system – indeed, it is the system that almost all clients use in every other area of their business.

In a nutshell, happier clients, agreed bills, fewer write offs and much greater clarity of scope and responsibility were the results of adopting effective project management processes in the firm.

Kevin Doolan and Paul Smith are partners at Eversheds LLP. They can be contacted at: kevindoolan@eversheds.com and paulsmith@eversheds.com, respectively

Case study 4: Seyfarth Shaw LLP – Building an effective service delivery programme for clients

By Robert Reynolds, partner, Seyfarth Shaw LLP

AS LEGAL fees have continued to rise over the last decade, more and more of the large companies that procure large volume legal services from outside firms have joined a chorus of requests for more efficient delivery of such services. Seyfarth Shaw LLP (Seyfarth) is one of the law firms that has been a leader in responding to this trend. Seyfarth has developed a robust practice delivery programme that includes:

- Process management capabilities;
- Project management resources; and
- Programme development expertise.

As it has evolved, the programme has become known in and outside of Seyfarth as 'Seyfarth*Lean*' and has become an integral part of the Seyfarth culture.

In this case study, we will discuss the history of the Seyfarth service delivery programme, the application of process management and project management modules of the programme to two different client engagements, the practical results of the 'Seyfarth*Lean*' programme and some final conclusions.

The history of the programme

Seyfarth concluded in the middle of the last decade that clients were unlikely to continue to accept annual rate increases from their outside law firms in the future as easily as they had done in the past. After much reflection, Seyfarth concluded that the core of the concern presented by the clients related to the inherent inefficient nature of the hourly fee business model adopted by most law firms and their clients. Specifically, law firm revenues increase under this model as hours on the books go up and there is very little incentive towards efficiency in this model other than increasing client resistance to increasing fees.

Seyfarth concluded consequently that an appropriate response to the concerns presented by the clients must lie in shifting the legal service delivery model (and thus the business model) towards an approach that places a premium on efficiency. With that notion in mind, Seyfarth began to explore various efficiency methodology programmes that might be effectively applied to the practice of law.

After reviewing a number of approaches, Seyfarth determined that a 'Lean Six Sigma' based approach might be a compelling strategy for the development of the solution contemplated by Seyfarth. Seyfarth then initiated discussions with several clients that had experience with the application of Lean Six Sigma practices to their operating businesses and to their law departments to explore the possibility of the development of a Lean Six Sigma programme. With much encouragement from these clients, Seyfarth engaged an outside consultant to assist the firm with the development of the programme to build 'Seyfarth*Lean*'.

Seyfarth encountered a number of challenges in the development of the programme. For example, it learned quickly that pure Six Sigma relies significantly on mathematical computation of various data sets, statistical analysis and other calculations. Since many lawyers become lawyers specifically to cut out much of this kind of analysis from their professional life, Seyfarth had to determine how to provide enough flexibility in the Seyfarth*Lean* Six Sigma solution, to retain the data analysis that is an integral element of the Lean Six Sigma approach, without relying on the lawyers themselves to deliver this analysis.

After much trial and error and assimilation of lessons learned (in good Lean Six Sigma fashion), Seyfarth eventually settled on an adaptation of Lean Six Sigma that would work for its lawyers and for its clients. This capability became known as the process development module.

As part of this process, Seyfarth also determined that robust project management capabilities would facilitate the application of Lean Six Sigma strategies to various legal service lines and the delivery of efficiency gains to highly-complex legal projects. Seyfarth therefore developed concurrently a project management module, drawing on the capabilities of its existing project management resources that, until then, had principally handled internal projects within Seyfarth.

In the course of its interviews with its client base and others, Seyfarth also determined that many of its clients had an increasing interest in building and implementing internal efficiency programmes. In response to that perception, Seyfarth also built a programme development module to support clients in developing their own programmes.

At this point, Seyfarth had organised its programme into the process development module, the project management module and the programme development module. Taken together, Seyfarth delivered these capabilities to the market as 'Seyfarth*Lean*'.

The following presents two examples that explore the application of the first two modules of 'Seyfarth*Lean*' to two different client initiatives.

Applications of 'Seyfarth*Lean*'

The first of these examples involved the transition of a client's significant intellectual property (IP) portfolio from an incumbent provider to Seyfarth, which relied principally on the process development module, although it also brought in some parts of the project management module. The second example involved a complex cross-border re-organisation programme with a two-year timeframe that applied the 'Seyfarth*Lean*' project management module.

Example one – The process development module

Seyfarth was asked by a Fortune 500 retail products company (Retail Company) to be considered as the law firm to replace its incumbent counsel on a large IP workflow. The general counsel of Retail Company was one of the foremost Lean Six Sigma practitioners in the US, both in legal disciplines and in operating companies. The target workflow comprised a high volume of small IP units that required daily processing. The general counsel perceived that it was a very good candidate for a Lean Six Sigma approach and consequently had a strong interest in evaluating law firms in the US that could offer experience in Lean Six Sigma in applicable legal domains. As he developed a candidate list, the general counsel determined that only a very few firms had considered the application of Lean Six Sigma to legal workflows and that Seyfarth was perhaps the firm that had done the most work in that area. As it turned out, Seyfarth not only had developed the 'Seyfarth*Lean*' adaptation of Lean Six Sigma, but also had built specific process maps in the area of interest of the general counsel, and had converted most of its IP operations in that area into a 'Seyfarth*Lean*' sub-programme.

As a second criteria, the general counsel relationship was focused on the law firm's ability to work well with the client and adapt well to the law department's style. The general counsel and his team worked together with Seyfarth over the course of several months to determine whether there would be a good fit between client and law firm, and whether the 'Seyfarth*Lean*' programme would serve well to support the general counsel's proposed strategy for the target IP portfolio.

At the conclusion of the evaluation period, the general counsel and his team selected Seyfarth as the new firm to provide the relevant legal services for the target portfolio. Over the course of several months after the selection was announced, Retail Company and Seyfarth worked together to transition the entire in-scope IP portfolio with the support of Seyfarth's project management office.

Example two –The project management module

One of the largest financial groups in the world (Oak) completed an acquisition several years ago that significantly extended its geographic reach in a particular region. To secure regulatory approval of the transactions, Oak was required to complete a complex, cross-border re-organisation within a several year time span ('Project Acorn'). Although Oak has a robust internal project management office, these internal resources were primarily assigned to other Oak initiatives and would not be available for 'Project Acorn'. Oak concluded therefore that it would benefit from engaging outside project management resources to serve as the programme office for 'Project Acorn'. Oak was already in discussions with Seyfarth on other initiatives and suggested that Oak and Seyfarth evaluate Seyfarth's ability to provide the programme office for 'Project Acorn' through its project management module. After much discussion, Seyfarth was engaged to serve in this role.

The 'Project Acorn' team numbers more than 100 principal and part-time team members. The project requires the movement of several hundred millions of dollars in assets, the creation of several new regulated entities and hundreds of millions of dollars in capitalisation flow, and involves over five different countries organised into several different phases.

Seyfarth has provided the programme office support for almost a year and the project continues into next year. The principal function of the programme office is to sequence the vast number of activities required for successful performance of each phase, identify the critical path for each phase, determine the dependencies for each step of the critical path, support the organisation of the teams for the performance of each module in the critical path, develop appropriate reporting vehicles, structure team communications required for team performance and cover myriad other organisational and substantive activities. Notably, Seyfarth is not providing legal services in this engagement, although Seyfarth's understanding of the legal context is helpful to the effective performance of its role. Seyfarth supports the engagement with a lead programme director who has many years of experience in very large-scale transactions and a programme manager with extensive programme management training, credentials and experience.

Results

The 'Seyfarth*Lean*' programme has brought about positive results for Seyfarth. The practical results of the programme include:

- Over 150 process maps (and counting) across an array of legal disciplines;
- A much more robust legal project management capability that facilitates transaction workflow, milestone management and cost reduction;
- Opportunities to integrate efficiency programmes into client organisations that wish to develop such initiatives;
- Enhanced technology infrastructure that provides much more relevant data to clients on a real-time basis;
- Top to bottom programmatic training across all 'Seyfarth*Lean*' disciplines; and
- Much closer relationships with its client base.

Seyfarth is pleased with the commercial benefits offered by its 'Seyfarth*Lean*' programme to its clients to date. The programme can provide significant cost savings in outside counsel fees and material reductions in demand on internal resources for both continuing streams of legal activity and on large-scale projects that do not repeat on an ongoing basis. Additionally, the programme permits the client and Seyfarth to develop alternative pricing arrangements that are supported by appropriate data analytics, performance metrics and reporting capabilities. Furthermore, Seyfarth is able to assist its clients in developing their own internal efficiency programmes.

Robert Reynolds is partner at Seyfarth Shaw LLP. He can be contacted at: rreynolds@seyfarth.com

Case study 5: Royal Bank of Canada – A client's perspective on law firm pricing

By Tamara Vanmeggelen, senior counsel and Manju Jessa, senior counsel, Royal Bank of Canada

THE DAYS of legal work being considered unique and, therefore, untouched by economic realities are over. The Law Group at Royal Bank of Canada (RBC) like most other in-house legal teams, is under constant pressure to reduce costs. RBC's philosophy on legal expense is to obtain value for the services rendered, which is not necessarily a function of the amount of time spent by a firm. A firm that works inefficiently can deliver good results, but RBC will not be happy to over pay for the work product. A firm that will take the initiative to issue legal invoices that reflect the true value of work performed during a billing period will be considered as a progressive firm – a firm that understands the client's perspective on legal services delivery.

Working with external counsel to manage costs

David Allgood, general counsel and executive vice president at RBC has been instrumental in challenging RBC's Law Group to rethink how legal services can be obtained. The 'Designated Counsel List' was created in the effort to manage external legal spend. There is no guarantee of work for a firm on this list and there is generally one or more competing firms in each jurisdiction in any given matter category. However, it is RBC's objective to only retain firms on the 'Designated Counsel List' for all of its work.

RBC expects law firms on the list to keep up with RBC's processes which lead to greater efficiency and effectiveness and lower legal expenses. Knowledge gained from prior work with RBC can lead to firms not only delivering cost-efficient service but working more profitably for themselves.

Designated counsel are given specific guidelines and principles that have changed the enterprise culture of how RBC uses both internal and external legal resources. These principles and guidelines remain the cornerstone of RBC's continued evolution in managing legal spend. They include:

- A formal budget for any matter expected to be more than CAD$10,000 in legal fees within 30 days of the retainer. RBC's budget template focuses on a case plan where the costs are broken down by phases to ensure proper staffing levels (by both number of lawyers and the level of seniority) and allocation of work throughout the life of the file. RBC regards budgets to be a commitment on the part of the law firm and generally only approves an increase in a budget when there has been a change in the underlying assumptions or scope;
- RBC indexes all legal opinions obtained and requires approval of any legal research before it is conducted. Where possible, the opinions and precedent documents are shared with other law

firms conducting similar research. This represents a significant cost saving by not having to pay multiple times for the same work product;

- All firms retained by RBC are required to submit invoices through RBC's electronic billing (e-billing) system. Budget templates are entered directly into the e-billing system by the law firm and, once approved by RBC, will be tracked against each invoice submitted to ensure fees remain within budget. The docket codes in the e-billing system (UTBMS standard codes) correlate to the budget template;
- Internal buyers of legal services are expected to match complexity of risk of a matter to expertise and expense of the external law firm; and
- Approved law firms have a senior partner assigned as relationship manager, who acts as a main contact point for RBC. The relationship manager or other senior lawyers in the firm will be called upon to ensure the right number and level of professionals work on each retainer.

Alternative Fee Arrangements (AFAs)

A model that creates strategic partnerships is based on the principle that the more work a law firm does for RBC, the more understanding that law firm will have of RBC's expectations on delivery of matters. The law firm will also have a better knowledge of how recurring work should be done to deliver a high degree of value at a lower cost. The lowest hourly rate does not mean the lowest cost, so driving down the hourly rates of preferred law firms only goes so far. Law firms that take the initiative in providing AFAs – particularly fixed fees – will tend to be retained more often by RBC. Effective project management will enable a law firm to deliver on these AFAs while remaining profitable.

Accordingly, RBC has done extensive research on alternative billing methods and has used most of them to varying degrees. Our experience with some of the pricing models used by law firms is summarised further.

Bonus arrangements

On more complex litigation matters, RBC has used the 'skin-in-the-game' model, where RBC holds back an agreed percentage on each invoice submitted. The percentage is to be earned by the firm only in the event that it achieves a pre-determined outcome, with a potential bonus for exceptional results measured on the basis of time to resolution and result. However, this model does not provide an incentive for a firm to be more efficient and inevitably results in additional negotiations, especially in situations where a large number of parties are involved, there are numerous deviations of outcomes and the quality of the results or duration of the case are not defined well enough (for example, if the litigation is settled at mediation with outstanding issues that require additional work for several more months).

Block flat fees

To manage legal expenses in high-volume auto-insurance claims litigation, RBC built a programme with input from external firms that allows firms to increase profitability due to greater efficiency by charging on a cost-per-file basis.

RBC allows firms to bid on a fixed annual flat fee based on a block of files within a geographic area and jurisdiction in increments of ten (i.e. CAD$XXX for ten files or CAD$YYY for 50 files). There is no minimum or maximum block that each firm bids on. This provides smaller firms an equal chance to bid with larger firms. The block of files have a pre-defined mix of complexity (based on low, medium and high risk ratings set by RBC) and the flat fee includes preparation for trial or arbitration, but allows for a supplemented payment if a hearing/arbitration occurs. The bid is renewed annually and firms can exit at anytime and have their files re-assigned. Six firms currently participate in this arrangement.

Fixed fee by phase/task

RBC has used fixed-fee arrangements throughout a certification motion on class-action litigation and by phases/tasks. For example, RBC retained a law firm in Europe to assist in the launch of a new credit product in a particular market. RBC and the firm collaborated to develop a work plan based on agreed assumptions, and the firm was then able to provide a staffing model and fixed fee for the retainer.

The right pricing model for RBC

RBC's most successful pricing models include a structure where fees are fixed and competition within the model still exists to ensure continued diligence on the part of the external firm over time. This provides a true incentive for firms to work more efficiently and continue on the same level of profitability – a win for both the firm and the client. Some examples are provided further.

Innovative ways of working – Using portals and 'Lean Six Sigma'

Technology has been a leading driver of new ways to manage external legal expenses along with the infiltration of process management concepts developed in the manufacturing sector.

Our collections residential mortgage enforcement model is a good example of how technology can be used to reduce costs. Seven law firms performing mortgage enforcement work for RBC agreed to share best practices, develop a common portal to enable RBC to follow each file virtually, produce aggregate reports (for RBC use only) and enter into a highly-specialised alternative billing arrangement based on fixed fees per task. These netted out costs which firms agreed to absorb and volume discounts in exchange for exclusive rights to continue mortgage enforcement work in the respective jurisdictions. This programme has been one of RBC's most successful examples of competing firms working together for the benefit of a common client, and efficiencies have been gained throughout the years as a result of it.

The portal which is the law firm's virtual file contains every note and document attached to the file, and is open to RBC (but not to other firms participating). By having RBC looking in on every file, the firms benefit by enhancing communication, performance and quality. Efficiency is also achieved as the need for RBC to contact law firms for file updates is eliminated and RBC is able to easily compare firms on performance, results and overall cost.

The RBC Law Group has also undertaken a formal Lean Six Sigma programme with one of its external counsel, to improve the process of employment-related complaints and litigation. The tasks are documented on the initial process map and great improvements in efficiency and communication have been achieved by agreeing on a defined process for a file flow, instructions and communication.

The Lean Six Sigma programme is paving the way to the development of template letters, pleadings, reports and an AFA based on fixed fees per task. RBC hopes to leverage this experience across other areas of commercial litigation.

Outsourcing

RBC considers outsourcing to be an important component of managing legal expenses. There is a wide variety of tasks appropriate for outsourcing but, to date, RBC has outsourced routine contract review and risk assessment, various stages of documentary discovery and jurisdictional opinion work. Accordingly, RBC has used various Legal Process Outsourcing (LPO) firms and will continue to explore further areas of work to outsource.

Price structures vary from hourly rates to price per page or document. RBC has had positive experiences with LPO firms both onshore and offshore, but recommends that all price estimates be fully explored for excluded costs and underlying assumptions as they could dramatically change cost estimates (i.e. average size and format of document in a price-per-document pricing, parameters set by the client for coding breakdown, amount of paper *versus* electronic documents, source of documents, etc.) All these factors give rise to extra costs to convert the documents before using e-discovery software. To effectively predict the costs, a project plan for the documentary discovery phase of litigation (preferably including opposing counsel) is paramount to ensuring that cost and time are not wasted.

RBC has also had success with outsourcing internal legal and risk assessment review with respect to a certain type of contract to an offshore LPO. RBC and the LPO firm built a workflow and process to achieve consistent quality of output. What is special about this ongoing programme is that the review conducted by offshore lawyers encompasses not only routine legal review, but also a risk assessment for use by RBC. The risk parameters were defined by RBC but legal common sense comes into play. This project dispels the myth that outsourcing is only for the mundane legal tasks. With the right LPO firm, the work can evolve into much more robust long-term projects.

The LPO firm provides access to its web-based software where RBC uploads documents daily for an overnight turnaround time. Due to large volumes of work on a daily basis, the fees are based on a full-time equivalent salary rate, rather than the cost per document. This outsourcing arrangement has saved RBC substantial costs and has freed up its internal resources to work on higher priority and more complex matters.

The importance of communication

Active management of all retainers is an important part of managing legal expenses. RBC has had a variety of experiences dealing with law firms which are not yet able to provide a consistent quality of matter management. The way a firm responds to missteps is important.

For example, RBC retained a top tier law firm to perform a transaction on a fixed-fee basis. The work was done and the bill received was more than twice the amount that was originally quoted. After inquiring about this, RBC was told that the work was not as straightforward as the law firm originally believed and that additional research was required. The law firm did not inform RBC in advance until after RBC received the invoice and made the inquiry. The law firm believed that the bill was appropriate given the quality of the work done. After much discussion, we agreed to pay 20 per cent (rather than 50 per cent) above the agreed fee cap. Although this represented a concession by the law firm of 30 per cent of the overrun, we remained extremely dissatisfied. As a result of this experience, we have been using other firms on the 'Designated Counsel List'.

In contrast to this, RBC retained another law firm, again on a fixed-fee basis. During the engagement, RBC provided additional instructions and, as a result, the project went over budget. The law firm knew that the additional work was out of scope, but in an effort to provide good service, the work was completed without question and without informing RBC that it added the additional cost. The partner from the law firm called and told us that the final bill was 40 per cent over the cap. He explained that he would not charge us the excess since the cap was agreed to and because RBC was not informed that the new work was out of scope. The partner was able to list the out-of-scope work and asked us to consider whether we had received good value. He asked us to consider if there was any portion of the work that we were prepared to pay for. In the end, RBC agreed to pay what was determined to be the overage for the out-of-scope work, which amounted to an additional fee (17 per cent above the original fixed fee). RBC now uses this law firm (and that particular partner) as the preferred provider for that jurisdiction.

Similarly, in Latin America, RBC hired a firm to register a few entities so that business could be done with ease in that jurisdiction. The firm had to stick to its original budget for regulatory filing work when it presented a bill for a higher amount. The firm readily agreed as it had not sought the required pre-approval to go over budget. RBC had a good experience with this firm in terms of the quality of work and resolving the billing issue. For annual regulatory renewals, the firm prepared templates and implemented a process to enable it to perform the work more efficiently. RBC retained the firm for subsequent annual renewals for a fixed fee.

A mutually-beneficial partnership

By establishing a 'Designated Counsel List' and providing a set of guidelines and principles, it is RBC's goal to achieve strong, long-term relationships with its preferred firms – those that adopt efficient ways of working and so are able to lower the overall cost of legal expense for RBC. RBC has proved that these goals are not mutually exclusive and, in fact, complement one another. Firms which can achieve efficiency in file execution and superior results, combined with the creativity to value their services beyond a billable hour, will succeed with their corporate clients. Stronger relationships mean law firms have better-trained associates and more retainers, as well as the opportunity to help their clients with temporary secondments. Stronger relationships also mean that conflicts and concerns can be resolved more quickly and amicably. RBC views its relationships with firms on the 'Designated Counsel List' to be a partnership that it values and continuously seeks to build.

Both in Canada and internationally, RBC has not found that many firms are able to proactively deliver unique value propositions without prompting. A law firm that can provide fee estimates at the start of a matter, regardless of whether or not they were asked for, makes it simpler for in-house counsel to identify the law firms which are truly geared up to deliver matters based on value of the work. RBC, like many other large buyers of legal services, is using this as a differentiator in retaining external counsel. RBC is hopeful from the examples it has seen to date that more firms will re-evaluate the way they deliver legal services and find alternative ways to maintain profitability beyond the billable hour. This will assist RBC and other corporations to achieve their internal goals of cost management while building lasting strategic partnerships.

Tamara Vanmeggelen and Manju Jessa are senior counsel at the Royal Bank of Canada. They can be contacted at: tamara.vanmeggelen@rbc.com and manju.jessa@rbc.com

PART THREE

Appendices

Appendix 1: An asset purchase Gantt chart

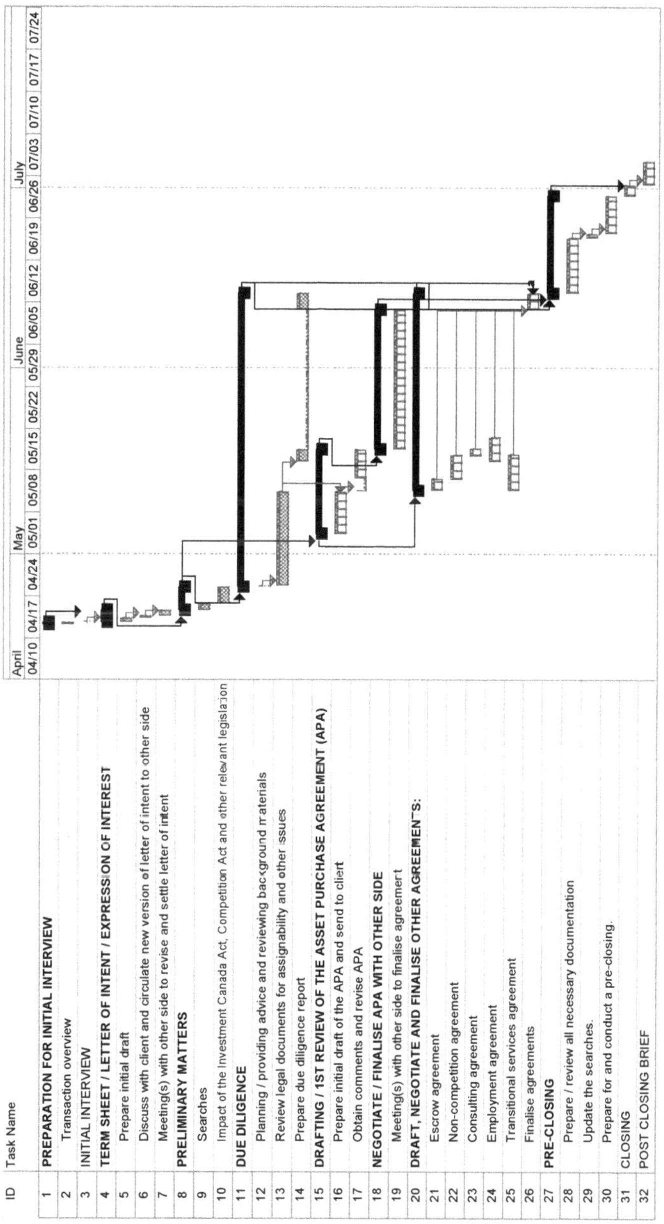

Appendix 2: A generic work plan

	Key Assumptions	Certainty Factor (%)	Total	Hours Estimate: Equity Partner	Non-Equity Partner	Counsel	Senior Associate (5+)	Mid Level Associate (3-4)	Junior Associate (1-2)	Student	Paralegal/ Clerk/ Other	External Resources
Summary of Time		**N/A**	0.0 hrs	0.0 hrs	0.0 hrs	0.0 hrs	0.0 hrs	0.0 hrs	0.0 hrs	0.0 hrs	0.0 hrs	0.0 hrs
PHASE 1			0.0 hrs									
Task A			0.0 hrs									
Task B			0.0 hrs									
Task C			0.0 hrs									
Task D			0.0 hrs									
Task E			0.0 hrs									
Task F			0.0 hrs									
PHASE 2			0.0 hrs									
Task A			0.0 hrs									
Task B			0.0 hrs									
Task C			0.0 hrs									
Task D			0.0 hrs									
Task E			0.0 hrs									
Task F			0.0 hrs									
PHASE 3			0.0 hrs									
PHASE 4			0.0 hrs									
PHASE 5			0.0 hrs									
PHASE 6			0.0 hrs									
PHASE 7			0.0 hrs									
PHASE 8			0.0 hrs									
PHASE 9			0.0 hrs									
PHASE 10			0.0 hrs									

Appendix 3: A work plan for an asset purchase

	Key Assumptions	Certainty Factor %	Total Hours	Hours Estimate						
				Equity Partner	Non-Equity Partner	Senior Associate (5+)	Mid Level Associate (3-4)	Junior Associate (1-2)	Paralegal / Clerk	Student
SUMMARY OF TIME		**59%**	510.0 hrs	108.0 hrs	0.0 hrs	2.5 hrs	218.0 hrs	102.0 hrs	6.5 hrs	73.0 hrs
PREPARATION FOR INITIAL INTERVIEW										
Transaction overview		80%	4.0 hrs	2.0 hrs			2.0 hrs			
INITIAL INTERVIEW		80%	0.5 hrs	0.5 hrs						
TERM SHEET / LETTER OF INTENT / EXPRESSION OF INTEREST										
Prepare initial draft		80%	4.9 hrs	1.4 hrs			3.5 hrs			
Discuss with client and circulate new version of letter of intent to other side		80%	4.3 hrs	1.8 hrs			2.5 hrs			
Meeting(s) with other side to revise and settle letter of intent	Assume 3 calls	80%	8.8 hrs	3.8 hrs			5.0 hrs			
PRELIMINARY MATTERS										
Initiate searches and obtain the written authorisation for release of information and the relevant government account numbers.		80%	7.0 hrs	1.0 hrs			2.0 hrs		4.0 hrs	
Consider the impact of the Investment Canada Act, Competition Act and other relevant legislation upon the transaction.		90%	4.0 hrs	2.0 hrs			2.0 hrs			
DUE DILIGENCE										
Planning / providing advice in relation to the due diligence process and reviewing background materials		80%	4.0 hrs	3.5 hrs		0.5 hrs				
Review legal due diligence documents for assignability and other issues	Assumes 100 contracts	50%	85.0 hrs	3.0 hrs		2.0 hrs	5.0 hrs	25.0 hrs		50.0 hrs
Prepare due diligence report		70%	20.0 hrs	2.0 hrs			3.0 hrs	15.0 hrs		
DRAFTING / 1ST REVIEW OF THE ASSET PURCHASE AGREEMENT (APA)										
Prepare initial draft of the APA and send to client		70%	39.0 hrs	14.0 hrs			20.0 hrs	5.0 hrs		
Obtain comments and revise APA		70%	20.5 hrs	7.5 hrs			13.0 hrs			
NEGOTIATE / FINALISE APA WITH OTHER SIDE										
Meeting(s) with other side to finalise agreement	Assume 4 meetings with other side + 2 client meetings	50%	133.0 hrs	45.0 hrs			78.0 hrs	10.0 hrs		
DRAFT, NEGOTIATE AND FINALISE OTHER AGREEMENTS:										
Escrow agreement	Bespoke agreement required	50%	8.0 hrs	1.0 hrs			7.0 hrs			
Non-competition agreement	Bespoke agreement required	50%	8.0 hrs	1.0 hrs			7.0 hrs			
Consulting agreement	Bespoke agreement required	50%	8.0 hrs	1.0 hrs			7.0 hrs			
Employment agreement	Bespoke agreement required	50%	16.0 hrs	2.0 hrs			14.0 hrs			
Transitional services agreement	Bespoke agreement required	50%	16.0 hrs	2.0 hrs			14.0 hrs			
PRE-CLOSING										
Prepare / review all necessary documentation		60%	57.0 hrs	7.0 hrs			20.0 hrs	30.0 hrs		
Update the searches		80%	4.0 hrs	0.5 hrs			1.0 hrs		2.5 hrs	
Prepare for and conduct a pre-closing		50%	34.0 hrs	4.0 hrs			8.0 hrs	12.0 hrs		10.0 hrs
CLOSING		90%	10.0 hrs	2.0 hrs			2.0 hrs	3.0 hrs		3.0 hrs
POST CLOSING BRIEF		80%	14.0 hrs				2.0 hrs	2.0 hrs		10.0 hrs

Appendix 4: A completed monitoring worksheet

Phase / Task		Assumptions	% work completed	Budget cost	Earned Value	Actual cost	Cost variance	Reason for variance
PREPARATION FOR INITIAL INTERVIEW								
	Transaction overview		100%	$2,400	$2,400	$1,800	$600	
INITIAL INTERVIEW			100%	$350	$350	$300	$50	
TERM SHEET / LETTER OF INTENT / EXPRESSION OF INTEREST							$0	
	Prepare initial draft		100%	$2,730	$2,730	$2,200	$530	
	Discuss with client and circulate new version of letter of intent to other side		100%	$2,510	$2,510	$2,000	$510	
	Meeting(s) with other side to revise and settle letter of intent	Assume 3 calls	100%	$5,125	$5,125	$3,875	$1,250	only required 2 calls
PRELIMINARY MATTERS								
	Initiate searches and obtain the written authorisation for release of information and the relevant government account numbers.		100%	$2,900	$2,900	$2,000	$900	
	Consider the impact of the Investment Canada Act, Competition Act and other relevant legislation upon the transaction.		100%	$2,400	$2,400	$3,000	-$600	Additional senior partner time required to determine relevance
DUE DILIGENCE								
	Planning / providing advice in relation to the due diligence process and reviewing background materials		100%	$2,725	$2,725	$2,100	$625	
	Review legal due diligence documents for assignability and other issues	Assume 100 contracts	100%	$28,200	$28,200	$33,500	-$5,300	118 contracts reviewed
	Prepare due diligence report		100%	$8,900	$8,900	$6,875	$2,025	
DRAFTING / 1ST REVIEW OF THE ASSET PURCHASE AGREEMENT (APA)								
	Prepare initial draft of the APA and send to client		100%	$21,800	$21,800	$22,750	-$950	
	Obtain comments and revise APA		100%	$11,750	$11,750	$10,000	$1,750	
NEGOTIATE / FINALISE APA WITH OTHER SIDE								
	Meeting(s) with other side to finalise agreement	Assume 4 meetings with other side + 2 client meetings	100%	$74,500	$74,500	$65,000	$9,500	only required 3 meetings with other side and 1 client meeting
DRAFT, NEGOTIATE AND FINALISE OTHER AGREEMENTS:								
	Escrow agreement	Bespoke agreement required	90%	$4,200	$3,780	$4,100	-$320	Agreement more complicated than expected
	Non-competition agreement	Bespoke agreement required	75%	$4,200	$3,150	$4,000	-$850	Underestimated effort
	Consulting agreement	Bespoke agreement required	85%	$4,200	$3,570	$6,200	-$2,630	Assumed only 1 agreement, was actually 3 different agreements
	Employment agreement	Bespoke agreement required	25%	$8,400	$2,100	$2,000	$100	
	Transitional services agreement	Bespoke agreement required	0%	$8,400	$0	$0	$0	
PRE-CLOSING								
	Prepare / review all necessary documentation		0%	$26,900	$0	$0	$0	
	Update the searches.		0%	$1,600	$0	$0	$0	
	Prepare for and conduct a pre-closing.		0%	$14,100	$0	$0	$0	
CLOSING			0%	$4,350	$0	$0	$0	
POST CLOSING BRIEF			0%	$4,300	$0	$0	$0	
			72%	$246,940	$178,890	$171,700	$7,190	

Appendix 5: A sample staffing profile

	Hour range		% of total
Equity partner	108 to	152hrs	21%
Non-equity partner	-	-	0%
Senior associate	3 to	4 hrs	0%
Mid-level associate	218 to	307hrs	43%
Junior associate	102 to	144hrs	20%
Clerk paralegal	7 to	9 hrs	1%
Student	73 to	103hrs	14%
Total	**510 to**	**719hrs**	**100%**

Appendix 6: A sample change request form

Client / matter number:	<enter the client/matter number>
Change ID number:	<assign a number so the change can be referred to in future reports>
Title of change:	<provide a brief title of the change for reference purposes>
Origination date:	<date the change was requested or documented>
Originator:	<the name of the individual or organisation requesting the change>
Priority:	<Critical, High, Medium, Low>
Reason for change:	<identify the reasons for the change and the consequences and/or risks of rejecting the change>
Impact on budget:	<identify the expected impact on the budget>
Impact on schedule:	<identify the expected impact on the schedule>
Impact on resources:	<identify the expected impact on resources>
Status of change:	<Approved, Pending, Postponed, Rejected>
Decision made by:	<identify who made the decision regarding the change>
Date decision made:	<identify the date the decision was made>

Index

www.ingramcontent.com/pod-product-compliance
Ingram Content Group UK Ltd.
Pitfield, Milton Keynes, MK11 3LW, UK
UKHW050231160926
8657IPUK00008B/192

9 781907 787614